D0996050

QUICHES
FLANS & TARTS

MARY NORWAK

QUICHES
FLANS & TARTS

WARD LOCK LIMITED · LONDON

© Mary Norwak 1985

First published in Great Britain in 1985
by Ward Lock Limited, 82 Gower Street,
London WC1E 6EQ.

All Rights Reserved. No part of this publication
may be reproduced, stored in a retrieval system,
or transmitted, in any form or by any means,
electronic, mechanical, photocopying, recording,
or otherwise, without the prior permission of the
Copyright owners.

Text filmset in Goudy Old Style
by HBM Typesetting, Chorley, Lancs.
Printed and bound in Italy by Sagdos SpA.

British Library Cataloguing in Publication Data

Norwak, Mary
    Quiches, flans and tarts.
    1. Flans (Cookery)
    I. Title
    641.8   TX773

ISBN 0-7063-6378-7

CONTENTS

Acknowledgements

Cover photograph by Eric Carter

Inside photography by Peter Myers

Home Economist   Clare Gordon-Smith assisted by Alison Gaskin

Stylist   Alison Williams

Line drawings by Peter Mennim

The author and publisher would like to thank the following companies for sponsoring photographs:

Blue Nun (page 17); Cheeses from Switzerland (page 41); John West Foods Ltd (page 69) **and** Perrier (page 29).

Notes

It is important to follow the metric, imperial or American measures when using the recipes in this book. Do not use a combination of measures.

American terminology within recipes is indicated by the use of brackets in both the list of ingredients and in the method.

American measures which follow metric and imperial measures within the recipe methods are preceded by the term 'US'.

INTRODUCTION

The word *quiche* has become sadly debased over the past few years, and an anglicized *Quiche Lorraine* bears little resemblance to the true French version of a light puffy case containing cubes of mild bacon in a rich egg and cream custard. Today, there are curious mixtures in solid pastry cases (shells), thick with cheese and heavily garnished with tomatoes, which bear no resemblance to the subtle airiness of the true *quiche*. The British version is a flan, with a name derived from the medieval word *flawn*. The word *tart* is also used for sweet recipes, when a pie does not have a lid, but there is a further problem since this is known as a *pie* in America.

Whichever word you choose to employ, this book contains over one hundred recipes, both savoury and sweet, including many traditional French favourites. Quiches, flans or tarts should not be an excuse for using up leftovers, but small quantities of ingredients can be extended to make a filling meal, with the addition of a sauce or custard. The rich custard is an important part of the majority of quiches, and there should be no skimping of ingredients. The combination of eggs and cream will give a rich smoothness to the filling, which cannot be achieved by using milk or by cutting down on eggs. The use of cream need not make a quiche particularly expensive, as the rest of the ingredients may be just a few vegetables from the garden or a little sharp cheese.

A quiche or flan may be used as a main course with an accompanying or following salad, or as a starter. A tart makes a pleasant finish to a meal, and can usually be prepared well in advance. Always remember, though, that these pastry dishes are at their best when freshly baked. In each recipe, I have recommended whether they should be served hot or cold, or whether they are better when just warm – a point of some importance to get the best from such simple yet delicious dishes.

I have also kept to one size for savoury quiches and flans, and to a slightly smaller size for sweet tarts, so that there is no need to keep a huge range of tins (pans) in the cupboard. The recommended size will feed 4–6 people, according to appetite and the rest of the meal. A larger size is suggested for party dishes, which will feed 12 people.

ALL THE BASICS

A really successful quiche, flan or tart depends on the quality of the pastry and filling ingredients, the choice of the right baking tin (pan), the care which is taken in lining and finishing the pastry case (shell), and, finally, the correct oven temperature and timing.

The pastry may be home-made, frozen or prepared from a packet mix. Certainly where puff pastry is concerned, many cooks do not want to be bothered with the amount of time and care involved, and all types of commercially prepared pastry can be used successfully, so the choice is entirely with the individual cook. Basic pastry recipes are given on pages 10–13.

EQUIPMENT

The container used for baking is of the greatest importance. There is no doubt that metal is best since it conducts heat quickly and ensures a golden crisp finish for pastry. The most professional implement to use is a simple hoop of metal placed on a baking sheet, but this can be difficult for an inexperienced cook to handle. There are many good flan tins (pie pans) available with removable bases, and these are very easy to use. If you lack the confidence to lift a large flan from a baking sheet or the base of a flan tin (pie pan), it can safely remain on the base when serving it.

Flan rings and tins (pans) range in size from about 15cm/ 6 inches to 32.5cm/13 inches which is about the largest size which can be placed in an ordinary household oven, and which can be used without risk of breakages. Individual flans and tarts may be prepared in Yorkshire pudding tins which come in sets of four to a sheet. Tiny quiches for drinks parties may be prepared in jam tart tins (patty pans). Quiches, flans and tarts should never be prepared on flat enamel or foil plates as the filling will be very thin. They may, however, be prepared in deep flan dishes made in foil, and suitable for freezer use.

INGREDIENTS

Plain (all purpose) flour is best for pastry making, and should be sifted before use. A pinch of salt brings out the flavour of pastry. Butter gives a good flavour, but melts very quickly at pastry-baking temperatures, and does not give the crisp flakiness which is needed for a good flan. The flavour is, however, best for sweet shortcrust pastry (sweet pie pastry) which has a more crumbly texture. Lard (shortening) gives a flaky pastry, while hard-block margarine gives a good crisp result because it does not collapse at high temperatures like butter. For everyday use, choose a mixture of lard (shortening) and hard-block margarine which will combine the best qualities of both fats. Soft margarine is for cake-making and should not be used for pastry.

Note Pastry types can be alternated, as liked, from those indicated in the recipes on pages 10–13.

RUBBING-IN (CUTTING-IN)

When pastry is made by hand, it is rubbed in (cut in) to combine fat and flour, ie the flour and cut-up fat are passed through the fingertips until the mixture resembles fine breadcrumbs. The temperature of the fat is important, as very hard or very soft fat does not rub in (cut in) evenly. For good results, use fat at room temperature (18°–21°C/65°–70°F) when the consistency is firm but just spreadable.

MIXERS AND FOOD PROCESSORS

Pastry may be made successfully with a mixer or food processor. If using a mixer, prepare on a low speed to avoid a mess, and be careful not to overmix. When using a food processor, only mix ingredients until a ball of dough is formed, then stop the machine at once, otherwise the pastry will be overmixed.

Note When using either machine, add most of the liquid to the pastry, but keep a little in reserve as the swift action of the machines tends to make the pastry a little sticky, and the full quantity of liquid may not be needed.

CHILLING

Coldness is essential for good pastry, and the warmth of the hands can make it difficult to roll out pastry and line tins. Chill the ball of pastry for 15–20 minutes in a refrigerator before rolling it. Wrap it in foil or clingfilm (plastic wrap) before chilling so that a skin does not form. When the pastry has been rolled and the tin (pan) lined, cover and chill again for 20–30 minutes before baking. The pastry will be less likely to shrink and slip down under the filling if this precaution is taken.

LINING A FLAN TIN (PIE PAN)

Place a flan ring on a baking sheet; or use a flan tin (pie pan) with a removable base. Roll out the pastry into a circle about 5cm/2 inches larger than the flan ring or tin (pan). To lift the pastry, loosely roll it round the rolling-pin or fold in half and then fold again. Lift into the flan tin (pie pan) or ring, and unroll or unfold. Ease carefully into shape with the hands without pulling or stretching. Start in the middle and work to the sides of the flan tin (pie pan) to push out air under the base. Press the pastry right into the sides of the tin (pan) with a finger, being careful not to crack the pastry. Roll across the top by pressing heavily with the rolling-pin to cut off surplus pastry. A plain flan edge is generally used for savoury fillings, and a fluted edge for sweet recipes.

BAKING

Quiches, flans and tarts may be baked with or without a filling. If the filling is very liquid, it is advisable to part-bake the pastry first to give a firm crisp base before adding the filling and continuing baking. Pre-heat the oven if necessary and put a flat metal baking sheet on the oven rack you intend using. This will become very hot, and if the flan tin (pie pan) is placed on top, the pastry will be sealed quickly and become beautifully crisp.

Baking pastry without a filling is known as *baking blind*. The simplest way to do this is to prick the pastry well so that air bubbles do not form underneath. Press in a piece of foil, and bake for the required time. If a golden base is needed and the flan case (pie shell) is not to be baked again with its filling, take out the foil and leave the pastry to bake for another 5 minutes. An alternative method is to line the pastry with foil or greaseproof (waxed) paper and fill with special china baking 'beans' or with dried beans, rice or crusts of bread. These are discarded after baking and the pastry browned before the filling is added.

The recipes in this book give cooking times, but because ovens vary, be prepared to add on another 5–10 minutes if necessary so that the pastry is lightly browned, and the filling set and golden. The cooked quiche or flan may be left on the base of the flan tin (pie tin), or eased off with a palette knife (metal spatula) on to a serving dish, but this takes a little practice. It is worth buying a flat serving dish, as ordinary dinner plates often have a slight well which may cause the pastry and filling to break.

DECORATIVE FINISHES

The pastry edge of a quiche or flan may be left completely plain. For a more professional finish, press the top edge of the pastry with the back of a fork, turning the prongs to the centre of the tin, and using the fork flat and turned at an angle of 45°. The edges may be nipped with a pair of tweezers, or crimped between thumb and first finger.

Surplus strips of pastry may be arranged in a lattice on sweet tarts. A plastic lattice maker may be used, over which the pastry is rolled, and which gives a neat and even lattice.

PREPARING AHEAD

Quiches, flans and tarts may be frozen for up to 4 weeks, but are never quite as delicious as when freshly baked. If you freeze them, thaw for 3 hours at room temperature and then re-heat if required. They can be re-heated in a microwave oven, but it is vital to remember that neither metal containers nor foil should be used. Follow manufacturer's instructions if in doubt.

If you have a time problem, prepare the pastry and line the flan tin (pie pan), then cover and keep in a refrigerator for up to 24 hours, until needed. Prepare all filling ingredients by chopping, slicing and pre-cooking if necessary, and store in a covered bowl in a refrigerator. Mix together liquid ingredients such as eggs and cream in a jug, and add seasoning; store in a refrigerator also. When the recipe is needed, it only takes a few minutes to assemble the ingredients for baking, so that the dish may be served freshly baked.

SHORTCRUST PASTRY
(BASIC PIE PASTRY)

Metric/imperial		American
175g/6 oz	plain (all-purpose) flour	1½ cups
1×2.5ml spoon/ ½ teaspoon	salt	½ teaspoon
40g/1½ oz	hard-block margarine, cut into small pieces	3 tablespoons
40g/1½ oz	lard, (shortening) cut into small pieces	3 tablespoons
2×15ml spoons/ 2 tablespoons	iced water	3 tablespoons
	flour for kneading and rolling out	

Sift together the flour and salt. Add the fat, and rub in (cut in) until the mixture resembles fine breadcrumbs. Add the water, and mix to a stiff dough. Turn on to a floured surface and knead lightly until smooth. Wrap in foil and chill for 30 minutes.

Roll out to the required shape and thickness, and line the flan tin. Chill for 30 minutes before use.

Notes 1) This amount of pastry will be enough for all savoury recipes using a 22.5cm/9 inch flan tin. It will also be enough for 12–15 party quiches and tartlets.
2) For 30cm/12 inch party quiches and flans, make 1½ recipe quantities.
3) The pastry may be frozen. Roll it out, form into a square, wrap in greaseproof (waxed) paper, then in foil or polythene, and freeze for up to 4 months. Thaw slowly, then cook as fresh pastry. Do not re-freeze in cooked form.

CHEESE PASTRY

Metric/imperial		American
175g/6 oz	plain (all-purpose) flour	1½ cups
1×2.5ml spoon/ ½ teaspoon	salt	½ teaspoon
	a pinch of pepper	
50g/2 oz	hard cheese, finely grated (see **Note**)	½ cup
40g/1½ oz	hard-block margarine, cut into small pieces	3 tablespoons
40g/1½ oz	lard, (shortening) cut into small pieces	3 tablespoons
	1 egg yolk	
1×5ml spoon/ 1 teaspoon	iced water	1 teaspoon
	flour for kneading and rolling out	

Sift together the flour, salt and pepper. Add the cheese, then rub in (cut in) the fat until the mixture resembles fine breadcrumbs. Add the egg yolk and water, and mix to a stiff dough. Turn out on to a floured surface and knead lightly until smooth. Wrap in foil and chill for 30 minutes. Continue as for Shortcrust Pastry (Basic Pie Pastry).

Notes 1) The cheese must be dry and finely grated, as a soft sticky cheese will not mix evenly and will make the pastry difficult to handle. Either a strongly flavoured cheese or a mixture will give a good flavour, eg Cheddar or Parmesan.
2) Cheese pastry is particularly good with a slightly bland filling, eg white fish or poultry.

WHOLEMEAL SHORTCRUST PASTRY
(WHOLEMEAL PIE PASTRY)

Metric/imperial		American
175g/6oz	81% wholemeal (wholewheat) **or** 81% and 100% wholemeal (wholewheat) flour, mixed	1½ cups
1×2.5ml spoon/ ½ teaspoon	salt	½ teaspoon
40g/1½oz	hard-block margarine, cut into small pieces	3 tablespoons
40g/1½oz	lard (shortening), cut into small pieces	3 tablespoons
2×15ml spoons/ 2 tablespoons (approx)	iced water	3 tablespoons (approx)
	flour for kneading and rolling out	

Sift together the flour and salt. Add the fat, and rub in (cut in) until the mixture resembles fine breadcrumbs. Add the water very gradually, and mix to a stiff dough. Turn out on to a floured surface and knead lightly until smooth. Wrap in foil and chill for 30 minutes.

Roll out more thickly than for Shortcrust Pastry (Basic Pie Pastry), then line the flan tin (pie pan). Chill for 30 minutes before use.

Notes 1) Add the water very carefully, as wholemeal (wholewheat) flour absorbs a lot of water, and too much will make the pastry very hard and tough.
2) The above quantity is enough for a 17.5–20cm/7–8 inch flan tin (pie pan). It is also enough for 9–10 party quiches and tartlets.
3) This pastry is particularly good for savoury fillings such as meat and sausage-meat, and for fruit fillings.

Variation
Sweet Wholemeal (Wholewheat) Pastry
Make as above, adding 1×5ml spoon/1 teaspoon sugar to the basic recipe.

PUFF PASTRY

Metric/imperial		American
450g/1 lb	plain (all-purpose) flour	4 cups
1×5ml spoon/ 1 teaspoon	salt	1 teaspoon
450g/1 lb	hard-block margarine	2 cups
2×5ml spoons/ 2 teaspoons	lemon juice	2 teaspoons
300ml/½ pint	iced water	1¼ cups
	flour for kneading and rolling out	

Sift together the flour and salt. Divide the margarine into four even pieces. Rub (cut) one piece into the flour, and mix to a pliable dough with lemon juice and water. Turn on to a floured surface and knead well until smooth. Leave in a cold place for 15 minutes.

Using two knives, form the remaining fat into a slab 12.5cm/5 inches square on a floured surface. Roll the dough into an oblong 27.5×15cm/11×6 inches. Place the slab of fat on the top end of the dough, leaving a margin of about 1.25cm/½ inch along the sides and top. Fold the rest of the dough over, placing the upper edges together. Brush off any surplus flour.

Turn the pastry round so that the folded edge is on the left-hand side. Press the three open edges together with a rolling-pin to seal. Press the dough across about five times with a rolling-pin to flatten. Roll out into an oblong about 30×15cm/ 12×6 inches, keeping the edges straight. Leave to rest in a refrigerator or cold place for 20 minutes before the second rolling.

Fold the pastry in three by folding the bottom third upwards and the top third downwards and over to cover it. Turn so that the folded edge is again on the left. Seal the edges well, and roll out as above. Fold, turn and seal the edges as before. Rest in a cold place for 20 minutes before the third rolling.

Roll out four more times, always turning and sealing the dough as above. Leave to rest for 20 minutes in a cold place between each rolling. If any patches of fat show, give the dough another rolling. Rest the dough before rolling out to the required thickness.

Notes 1) This recipe makes about 900g/2 lb pastry, but, as it is rather time-consuming, there is little point in making a smaller quantity. Surplus pastry may either be kept in a refrigerator or frozen as for Shortcrust Pastry (Basic Pie Pastry) on page 10.
2) This quantity will be enough for two 30cm/12 inch, three 20cm/8 inch quiches, flans and tarts, or 36–40 tiny quiches/ tartlets.
3) Recipes made with puff pastry are best eaten hot but can be eaten cold if freshly baked. They should not be prepared ahead.

SWEET SHORTCRUST PASTRY
(SWEET PIE PASTRY)

Metric/imperial		American
175g/6 oz	plain (all-purpose) flour	1½ cups
½ × 2.5ml spoon/ ¼ teaspoon	salt	¼ teaspoon
75g/3 oz	butter, cut into small pieces	6 tablespoons
25g/1 oz	caster sugar	2 tablespoons
	1 egg yolk	
1 × 15ml spoon/ 1 tablespoon	iced water	1 tablespoon
	flour for kneading and rolling out	

Sift together the flour and salt. Add the butter, and rub in (cut in) until the mixture resembles fine breadcrumbs. Stir in the sugar. Mix together the egg yolk and water, and add to the flour mixture. Mix to a firm dough. Knead lightly on a floured surface and form into a flattened ball. Wrap in foil and chill for 30 minutes. Continue as for Shortcrust Pastry (Basic Pie Pastry) on page 10.

Notes 1) This amount of pastry will be enough for all sweet recipes using a 20cm/8 inch flan tin (pie pan), with a small surplus to use for lattice trimming or other decoration. It will also be enough for 12–15 tartlets.

2) For 30cm/12 inch party tarts, double the recipe quantities so that the pastry will not be too thin and frail when rolled out. Surplus pastry may be used for decorations, or for a few small fruit or sweet tarts.

Finishes for Sweet Tarts

A fruit tart may be finished with a jam or jelly glaze, or with a meringue topping. When glazing a tart, spoon on the glaze, starting in the centre and working outwards. For a professional finish, use a small household paint brush about 2.5cm/1 inch wide, and brush on the glaze, also brushing a shine on to the pastry edging.

Use a golden glaze made from apricot jam for white, orange or green fruit, and a red glaze made from raspberry jam or red-currant jelly for red, purple or pink fruit.

APRICOT GLAZE

Add 4×15ml spoons/4 tablespoons/5 US tablespoons water and the juice of half a lemon to 450g/1 lb apricot jam. Bring slowly to the boil, simmer for 5 minutes, then sieve. Return to the pan and boil for 5 minutes, then brush on to the fruit while warm. The glaze may be stored in a jam jar for up to 1 month.

RASPBERRY GLAZE

Prepare as for Apricot Glaze, using raspberry jam.

REDCURRANT GLAZE

Beat some redcurrant jelly until well broken up. Strain into a pan and heat gently, stirring until clear; do not boil. Use while still warm.

MERINGUE TOPPINGS

Whisk the egg whites until stiff but not dry, and gradually beat in the sugar until well blended, allowing 50g/2 oz/¼ US cup caster or light soft brown sugar to each egg white. Cool the tart before topping with the meringue mixture. Spread on the meringue mixture evenly, peaking slightly into the centre, or pipe on with a decorative tube. Ensure that the meringue covers the filling completely and reaches right to the pastry. Bake in a warm oven, 160°C/325°F/Gas 3, for 15 minutes so that the outside is crisp and the inside still soft. The meringue will 'weep' if too much sugar is used or if it is too coarse. The topping will shrink and be tough if the oven temperature is too low.

CONFECTIONER'S CUSTARD

Metric/imperial		American
	2 eggs	
50g/2 oz	caster sugar	¼ cup
25g/1 oz	plain (all-purpose) flour	¼ cup
25g/1 oz	cornflour (cornstarch)	¼ cup
300ml/½ pint	milk	1¼ cups
	a few drops vanilla essence (extract)	

Beat together the eggs and sugar until thick and pale like whipped cream. Sift together the flour and cornflour (cornstarch), and mix with a little cold milk to make a smooth paste. Add the egg mixture, and beat until smooth. Heat the remaining milk until almost boiling. Pour on to the egg mixture, stirring all the time. Return to the pan and heat gently, stirring all the time until the mixture boils. Remove from the heat and add vanilla essence (extract) to taste. Cover with buttered greaseproof (waxed) paper, and leave until cold before using.

Note Vanilla-flavoured confectioner's custard is generally a base for a fruit tart.

Variations
1) Flavour with almond (extract) or coffee essence (strong black coffee) or with grated chocolate according to what the custard is accompanying. Dissolve the chocolate in the milk.
2) A lighter richer sauce may be made by folding an equal quantity of whipped cream into the custard.

OF EGGS AND CREAM

A quiche is traditionally a subtle mixture of eggs and cream which thickens to a light custard when baked in a pastry case (shell). A little mild bacon or cheese and seasoning makes the most simple quiche baked in shortcrust (basic pie) or puff pastry (the latter is preferable if served freshly baked and warm). Many variations are permissible, with the addition of vegetables, herbs, fish, poultry or meat, but it is important not to overload a quiche with too many different ingredients.

Gruyère cheese is particularly good for quiches since it is pale-coloured and melts easily into the savoury custard. For English tastes, the sharper flavours of Cheddar, Lancashire, Leicestershire and Stilton are favourites. A sprinkling of Parmesan cheese baked on top gives a rich flavour and a tempting golden colour to any filling.

QUICHE LORRAINE

Metric/imperial		American
275g/10 oz	prepared puff pastry	about ¾ lb
100g/4 oz	unsmoked bacon, rinds removed and diced	½ cup
75g/3 oz	cooked ham, chopped	⅓ cup
	4 eggs	
600ml/1 pint	single (light) cream	2½ cups
50g/2 oz	butter, cut into small pieces	¼ cup
	pepper	

Line a 22.5cm/9 inch flan tin (pie pan) with the pastry, then chill. Prick the pastry lightly with a fork.

Simmer the bacon in water for 15 minutes, then drain well. Mix the bacon and ham and sprinkle them into the pastry case (shell).

Beat together the eggs and cream lightly with the butter and pepper. Pour into the pastry case (shell) and bake in a hot oven, 220°C/425°F/Gas 7, for 10 minutes, then reduce the heat to fairly hot, 190°C/375°F/Gas 5, and bake for a further 30 minutes. Eat hot.

CALABRESE AND HAM QUICHE

Metric/imperial		American
275g/10 oz	prepared shortcrust pastry (basic pie pastry)	about ¾ lb
175g/6 oz	calabrese (broccoli)	⅓ lb
	salt, pepper	
25g/1 oz	butter	2 tablespoons
	1 medium onion, finely chopped	
175g/6 oz	cooked ham, diced	¾ cup
	3 eggs	
300ml/½ pint	single (light) cream	1¼ cups
75g/3 oz	Cheddar cheese, grated	¾ cup
25g/1 oz	Parmesan cheese, grated	¼ cup
	a pinch of ground nutmeg	

Line a 22.5cm/9 inch flan tin (pie pan) with the pastry, then chill. Prick the pastry well and bake blind in a fairly hot oven, 200°C/400°F/Gas 6, for 15 minutes. Leave to cool.

Cook the calabrese in boiling salted water until just tender, then drain thoroughly and slice thinly. Melt the butter in a pan and cook the onion until soft. Spread in the pastry case (shell) and cover with the ham and calabrese (broccoli).

Beat together the eggs and cream, then add the Cheddar cheese and plenty of salt and pepper. Pour the mixture over the ham and vegetables, and sprinkle with the Parmesan cheese and nutmeg. Bake in a fairly hot oven, 190°C/375°F/Gas 5, for 30 minutes. Eat hot or cold.

CURRIED HAM QUICHE

Metric/imperial		American
275g/10 oz	prepared shortcrust pastry (basic pie pastry)	about ¾ lb
225g/8 oz	cooked ham, finely chopped	1 cup
3×15ml spoons/ 3 tablespoons	soured cream	4 tablespoons
2×15ml spoons/ 2 tablespoons	mayonnaise	3 tablespoons
	salt, pepper	
½×2.5ml spoon/ ¼ teaspoon	mustard powder	¼ teaspoon
1×5ml spoon/ 1 teaspoon	curry powder	1 teaspoon
	2 eggs	
150ml/¼ pint	single (light) cream	⅔ cup

Line a 22.5cm/9 inch flan tin (pie pan) with the pastry, then chill. Prick the pastry well and bake blind in a fairly hot oven, 200°C/400°F/Gas 6, for 15 minutes. Leave to cool.

Mix the ham with the soured cream, mayonnaise, salt, pepper, mustard and curry powder, then spread this mixture into the pastry case (shell).

Beat together the eggs and cream, and pour into the pastry case (shell). Bake in a fairly hot oven, 190°C/375°F/Gas 5, for 30 minutes. Eat hot or cold.

Calabrese and Ham Quiche **and** Orange Cream Tart (page 56)

ASPARAGUS, GAMMON AND CHEESE QUICHE

Metric/imperial		American
275g/10 oz	prepared shortcrust pastry (basic pie pastry)	about ¾ lb
2 × 5ml spoons/ 2 teaspoons	prepared mustard	2 teaspoons
275g/10 oz	asparagus tips	scant ¾ lb
175g/6 oz	slice gammon (ham), diced	¾ cup
100g/4 oz	Gruyère cheese, thinly sliced	1 cup
	4 eggs	
150ml/¼ pint	single (light) cream	⅔ cup
	salt, pepper	
	a pinch of ground nutmeg	

Line a 22.5cm/9 inch flan tin (pie pan) with the pastry, then chill. Prick the pastry well and bake blind in a fairly hot oven, 200°C/400°F/Gas 6, for 15 minutes. Leave to cool.

Spread the mustard on the pastry base (shell). Cover with the asparagus tips, gammon (ham) and cheese. Beat together the eggs and cream, and season with salt, pepper and nutmeg. Pour this into the pastry case (shell) and bake in a fairly hot oven, 190°C/375°F/Gas 5, for 30 minutes. Eat hot or cold.

GRUYÈRE GAMMON QUICHE

Metric/imperial		American
275g/10 oz	prepared shortcrust pastry (basic pie pastry)	about ¾ lb
225g/8 oz	slice gammon (ham), cubed	½ lb
75g/3 oz	Gruyère cheese, cubed	¾ cup
	3 eggs	
150ml/¼ pint	single (light) cream	⅔ cup
	salt, pepper	
	a pinch of Cayenne pepper	
	a pinch of ground nutmeg	

Line a 22.5cm/9 inch flan tin (pie pan) with the pastry, then chill. Prick the pastry well and bake blind in a fairly hot oven, 200°C/400°F/Gas 6, for 15 minutes. Leave to cool.

Sprinkle the gammon (ham) and cheese into the pastry case (shell). Beat together the eggs and cream, and season well with salt, pepper, Cayenne pepper and nutmeg. Pour into the pastry case (shell) and bake in a fairly hot oven, 190°C/375°F/Gas 5, for 30 minutes. Eat hot or cold.

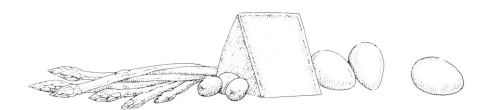

HAM AND COTTAGE CHEESE QUICHE

Metric/imperial		American
275g/10 oz	prepared shortcrust pastry (basic pie pastry)	about ¾ lb
225g/8 oz	cooked ham, minced (ground)	1 cup
175g/6 oz	cottage cheese	¾ cup
	3 eggs	
150ml/¼ pint	soured cream	⅔ cup
	salt, pepper	

Line a 22.5cm/9 inch flan tin (pie pan) with the pastry, then chill. Prick the pastry well and bake blind in a fairly hot oven, 200°C/400°F/Gas 6, for 15 minutes. Leave to cool.

Mix together the ham and cottage cheese. Beat together the eggs and cream, and blend into the mixture; season with salt and pepper. Pour the mixture into the pastry case (shell) and bake in a fairly hot oven, 190°C/375°F/Gas 5, for 30 minutes. Eat hot or cold.

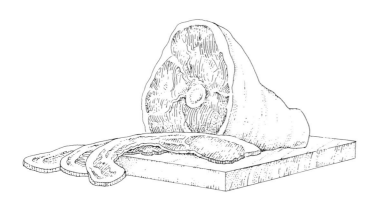

SPICED BACON AND EGG QUICHE

Metric/imperial		American
275g/10 oz	prepared shortcrust pastry (basic pie pastry)	about ¾ lb
	5 rashers back bacon (Canadian bacon slices), rinds removed and chopped	
150ml/¼ pint	single (light) cream	⅔ cup
	2 eggs **plus** 2 egg yolks	
½ × 2.5ml spoon/ ¼ teaspoon	Tabasco (hot pepper) sauce	¼ teaspoon
	a pinch of salt	
	a pinch of mustard powder	
75g/3 oz	Parmesan cheese, grated	¾ cup

Line a 22.5cm/9 inch flan tin (pie pan) with the pastry, then chill. Prick the pastry well and bake blind in a fairly hot oven, 200°C/400°F/Gas 6, for 15 minutes. Leave to cool.

Fry the bacon in a pan until the fat runs out and the bacon is just crisp. Drain well and sprinkle the bacon into the pastry case (shell).

Beat together the cream, eggs and egg yolks, and season with Tabasco (hot pepper) sauce, salt and mustard. Pour the mixture into the pastry case (shell) and sprinkle with the cheese. Bake in a fairly hot oven, 190°C/375°F/Gas 5, for 30 minutes. Eat hot or cold.

BACON AND POTATO QUICHE

Metric/imperial		American
275g/10 oz	prepared shortcrust pastry (basic pie pastry)	about ¾ lb
225g/8 oz	lean bacon, rinds removed and finely chopped	1 cup
225g/8 oz	potatoes, thinly sliced	½ lb
225g/8 oz	cooking apples, peeled, cored and thinly sliced	½ lb
	2 eggs	
300ml/½ pint	milk	1¼ cups
	pepper	

Line a 22.5cm/9 inch flan tin (pie pan) with the pastry, then chill. Prick the pastry well and bake blind in a fairly hot oven, 200°C/400°F/Gas 6, for 15 minutes. Leave to cool.

Arrange the bacon in the base of the pastry case (shell). Cover with the potatoes and then the apples. Beat together the eggs and milk, and season with pepper, then pour this over the apples. Bake in a fairly hot oven, 190°C/375°F/Gas 5, for 45 minutes. Eat hot.

BEEF AND HERB QUICHE

Metric/imperial		American
275g/10 oz	prepared shortcrust pastry (basic pie pastry)	about ¾ lb
	1 small onion, finely chopped	
	1 clove of garlic, crushed	
225g/8 oz	cooked beef, minced, (ground)	1 cup
25g/1 oz	Parmesan cheese, grated	¼ cup
	2 eggs	
4×15ml spoons/ 4 tablespoons	single (light) cream	5 tablespoons
	2 sage leaves, finely chopped	
1×5ml spoon/ 1 teaspoon	thyme	1 teaspoon
	salt, pepper	
	a pinch of Cayenne pepper	
	a pinch of ground nutmeg	

Line a 22.5cm/9 inch flan tin (pie pan) with the pastry, then chill. Prick the pastry well and bake blind in a fairly hot oven, 200°C/400°F/Gas 6, for 15 minutes. Leave to cool.

Sprinkle the onion and garlic into the pastry case (shell), and cover with the beef. Sprinkle with the cheese. Beat together the eggs and cream, and pour into the pastry case (shell). Sprinkle with the sage, thyme, salt, pepper, Cayenne pepper and nutmeg. Bake in a fairly hot oven, 190°C/375°F/Gas 5, for 30 minutes. Eat hot or cold.

CHICKEN AND PARSLEY QUICHE

Metric/imperial		American
275g/10 oz	prepared cheese pastry	about ¾ lb
450g/1 lb	cooked chicken, finely chopped	1 lb
8×15ml spoons/ 8 tablespoons	fresh parsley, chopped	9 tablespoons
	3 eggs	
300ml/½ pint	single (light) cream	1¼ cups
	salt, pepper	
	a pinch of ground nutmeg	
25g/1 oz	Parmesan cheese, grated	¼ cup

Line a 22.5cm/9 inch flan tin (pie pan) with the pastry, then chill. Prick the pastry well and bake blind in a fairly hot oven, 200°C/400°F/Gas 6, for 15 minutes. Leave to cool.

Mix the chicken with the parsley, and spread in the pastry case (shell). Beat together the eggs and cream, and season with salt, pepper and nutmeg. Pour this over the chicken, and sprinkle with the cheese. Bake in a fairly hot oven, 190°C/375°F/Gas 5, for 30 minutes. Eat hot.

CHICKEN, TONGUE AND LEEK QUICHE

Metric/imperial		American
275g/10 oz	prepared shortcrust pastry (basic pie pastry)	about ¾ lb
25g/1 oz	butter	2 tablespoons
	2 medium leeks, finely chopped	
100g/4 oz	cooked ox (beef) tongue, diced	½ cup
225g/8 oz	cooked chicken, diced	1 cup
	a pinch of marjoram	
	salt, pepper	
	2 eggs	
150ml/¼ pint	single (light) cream	⅔ cup

Line a 22.5cm/9 inch flan tin (pie pan) with the pastry, then chill. Prick the pastry well and bake blind in a fairly hot oven, 200°C/400°F/Gas 6, for 15 minutes. Leave to cool.

Melt the butter in a pan and cook the leeks until soft and golden. Stir in the tongue, chicken, marjoram, salt and pepper, then spread the chicken mixture in the pastry case (shell).

Beat together the eggs and cream, and pour this over the chicken. Bake in a fairly hot oven, 190°C/375°F/Gas 5, for 30 minutes. Eat hot or cold.

SALMON QUICHE

Metric/imperial		American
275g/10 oz	prepared shortcrust pastry (basic pie pastry)	about ¾ lb
15g/½ oz	butter	1 tablespoon
	1 medium onion, thinly sliced	
100g/4 oz	cooked salmon, flaked	½ cup
	2 eggs **plus** 1 egg yolk	
150ml/¼ pint	single (light) cream	⅔ cup
50g/2 oz	Gruyère **or** Cheddar cheese, grated	½ cup
	salt, pepper	
1 × 5ml spoon/ 1 teaspoon	chopped parsley	1 teaspoon

Line a 22.5cm/9 inch flan tin (pie pan) with the pastry, then chill. Prick the pastry well and bake blind in a fairly hot oven, 200°C/400°F/Gas 6, for 15 minutes. Leave to cool.

Melt the butter in a pan and cook the onion until soft. Stir in the salmon, and cook until the fish is just warmed through. Spread the mixture in the pastry case (shell).

Lightly beat together the eggs, egg yolk and cream, and pour this over the fish. Sprinkle with the cheese, seasoning and chopped parsley, and stir lightly to mix. Bake in a fairly hot oven, 190°C/375°F/Gas 5, for 30 minutes. Eat hot or cold.

TUNA QUICHE

Metric/imperial		American
275g/10 oz	prepared shortcrust pastry (basic pie pastry)	about ¾ lb
25g/1 oz	butter	2 tablespoons
	1 medium onion, finely sliced	
	1 medium green pepper, de-seeded and finely chopped	
100g/4 oz	button mushrooms, sliced	1 cup
200g/7 oz	canned tuna, drained and lightly mashed	7 oz
	12 capers, chopped	
	salt, pepper	
	3 eggs	
300ml/½ pint	milk	1¼ cups

Line a 22.5cm/9 inch flan tin (pie pan) with the pastry, then chill. Prick the pastry well and bake blind in a fairly hot oven, 200°C/400°F/Gas 6, for 15 minutes. Leave to cool.

Melt the butter in a pan and cook the onion, pepper and mushrooms until soft. Stir in the tuna, capers, salt and pepper, then remove from the heat. Beat together the eggs and milk, then blend into the fish.

Put the mixture into the pastry case (shell) and bake in a fairly hot oven, 190°C/375°F/Gas 5, for 30 minutes. Eat hot or cold.

SMOKED MACKEREL QUICHE

Metric/imperial		American
275g/10 oz	prepared shortcrust pastry (basic pie pastry)	about ¾ lb
25g/1 oz	butter	2 tablespoons
	1 large onion, finely chopped	
	3 large smoked mackerel fillets, flaked	
	3 eggs	
150ml/¼ pint	single (light) cream	⅔ cup
	salt, pepper	
	a few drops Tabasco (hot pepper) sauce	
25g/1 oz	Parmesan cheese, grated	¼ cup

Line a 22.5cm/9 inch flan tin (pie pan) with the pastry, then chill. Prick the pastry well and bake blind in a fairly hot oven, 200°C/400°F/Gas 6, for 15 minutes. Leave to cool.

Melt the butter in a pan and cook the onion until soft. Mix the mackerel with the onion, and spread in the pastry case (shell).

Beat together the eggs and cream, and season to taste with salt, pepper and Tabasco (hot pepper) sauce. Pour into the pastry case (shell), and sprinkle with the cheese. Bake in a fairly hot oven, 200°C/400°F/Gas 6, for 25 minutes. Eat cold.

SOLE AND SHRIMP QUICHE

Metric/imperial		American
275g/10 oz	prepared shortcrust pastry (basic pie pastry)	about ¾ lb
	1 large lemon sole (**or** flounder)	
175g/6 oz	peeled shrimps **or** prawns	1 cup
	grated rind of 1 lemon	
	salt, pepper	
75g/3 oz	Gruyère cheese, thinly sliced	¾ cup
	3 eggs	
300ml/½ pint	single (light) cream	1¼ cups
25g/1 oz	Parmesan cheese, grated	¼ cup

Line a 22.5cm/9 inch flan tin (pie pan) with the pastry, then chill. Prick the pastry well and bake blind in a fairly hot oven, 200°C/400°F/Gas 6, for 15 minutes. Leave to cool.

Poach the sole in water for 10 minutes, then remove the flesh and break into small pieces. Mix with the shrimps or prawns and the lemon rind, and season well with salt and pepper. Spread the mixture in the pastry case (shell), then arrange the cheese slices on top.

Beat together the eggs and cream, and pour this over the cheese. Sprinkle with the Parmesan cheese, and bake in a fairly hot oven, 200°C/400°F/Gas 6, for 10 minutes. Reduce the heat to moderate, 180°C/350°F/Gas 4, and bake for a further 25 minutes. Eat hot.

CRAB QUICHE

Metric/imperial		American
275g/10 oz	prepared shortcrust pastry (basic pie pastry)	about ¾ lb
225g/8 oz	crabmeat, flaked (see **Note**)	1 cup
50g/2 oz	Parmesan cheese, grated	½ cup
	salt, pepper	
1½×15ml spoons/ 1½ tablespoons	dry sherry	2 tablespoons
	2 eggs **plus** 1 egg yolk	
300ml/½ pint	single (light) cream	1¼ cups

Line a 22.5cm/9 inch flan tin (pie pan) with the pastry, then chill. Prick the pastry well and bake blind in a fairly hot oven, 200°C/400°F/Gas 6, for 15 minutes. Leave to cool.

Arrange the crabmeat in the pastry case (shell) and sprinkle with the cheese. Season with salt and pepper, and sprinkle with sherry. Beat together the eggs, egg yolk and cream, and pour this into the pastry case (shell). Bake in a fairly hot oven, 190°C/ 375°F/Gas 5, for 30 minutes. Eat hot or cold.

Note The crabmeat may be fresh, canned or frozen.

SEAFOOD QUICHE

Metric/imperial		American
275g/10 oz	prepared shortcrust pastry (basic pie pastry)	about ¾ lb
25g/1 oz	butter	2 tablespoons
	6 spring onions (scallions), chopped	
175g/6 oz	peeled prawns (shelled shrimp)	1 cup
225g/8 oz	cooked white fish, flaked	½ lb
	3 eggs	
150ml/¼ pint	single (light) cream	⅔ cup
6×15ml spoons/ 6 tablespoons	milk	7 tablespoons
40g/1½ oz	Gruyère cheese, grated	scant ½ cup
½×2.5ml spoon/ ¼ teaspoon	Tabasco (hot pepper) sauce	¼ teaspoon
	salt	

Line a 22.5cm/9 inch flan tin (pie pan) with the pastry, then chill. Prick the pastry well and bake blind in a fairly hot oven, 200°C/400°F/Gas 6, for 15 minutes. Leave to cool.

Melt the butter in a pan and cook the spring onions (scallions) until softened. Stir in the prawns and fish, then put the mixture in the pastry case (shell).

Beat together the eggs, cream, milk, cheese, Tabasco (hot pepper) sauce and salt, and pour this over the fish. Bake in a fairly hot oven, 190°C/375°F/Gas 5, for 30 minutes. Eat hot or cold.

Seafood Quiche

SCALLOP AND BACON QUICHE

Metric/imperial		American
275g/10 oz	prepared shortcrust pastry (basic pie pastry)	about ¾ lb
	6 scallops	
	6 rashers streaky bacon (bacon slices), rinds removed and finely chopped	
25g/1 oz	butter	2 tablespoons
	1 small onion, finely chopped	
4×15ml spoons/ 4 tablespoons	dry white wine	5 tablespoons
	salt, pepper	
	2 eggs	
150ml/¼ pint	single (light) cream	⅔ cup

Line a 22.5cm/9 inch flan tin (pie pan) with the pastry, then chill. Prick the pastry well and bake blind in a fairly hot oven, 200°C/400°F/Gas 6, for 15 minutes. Leave to cool.

Detach the red piece from the scallops. Cut the white part through to give two thin discs of flesh. Fry the bacon in a pan until the fat runs out and the bacon is just crisp. Add the scallops (white and red parts), and toss over low heat until golden. Drain off the bacon fat. Add the butter to the pan and stir in the onion. Continue cooking, stirring well until the onion is soft. Remove from the heat and stir in the wine. Season well with salt and pepper, then put the scallop mixture into the pastry case (shell).

Beat together the eggs and cream, and pour this over the scallops. Bake in a fairly hot oven, 190°C/375°F/Gas 5, for 30 minutes. Eat hot.

POTATO AND ANCHOVY QUICHE

Metric/imperial		American
275g/10 oz	prepared shortcrust pastry (basic pie pastry)	about ¾ lb
15g/½ oz	butter	1 tablespoon
	1 medium onion, finely chopped	
225g/8 oz	potatoes, diced	1⅓ cups
	3 eggs	
300ml/½ pint	single (light) cream	1¼ cups
75g/3 oz	Gruyère **or** Cheddar cheese, grated	¾ cup
75g/3 oz	anchovy fillets, drained	3 oz

Line a 22.5cm/9 inch flan tin (pie pan) with the pastry, then chill. Prick the pastry well and bake blind in a fairly hot oven, 200°C/400°F/Gas 6, for 15 minutes. Leave to cool.

Melt the butter in a pan and cook the onion until soft. Boil the potatoes until tender, then drain well. Arrange them in the pastry case (shell), and sprinkle with the cooked onion.

Beat together the eggs and cream, and pour this over the potatoes. Sprinkle with the grated cheese, and arrange the anchovy fillets on top. Bake in a fairly hot oven, 190°C/375°F/Gas 5, for 30 minutes. Eat hot.

GREEN OLIVE QUICHE

Metric/imperial		American
275g/10 oz	prepared shortcrust pastry (basic pie pastry)	about $\frac{3}{4}$ lb
40g/1½ oz	butter, melted	3 tablespoons
100g/4 oz	Gruyère cheese, thinly sliced	1 cup
	40 stuffed green olives	
	4 eggs	
300ml/½ pint	single (light) cream	1¼ cups
	salt, pepper	
25g/1 oz	Parmesan cheese, grated	¼ cup

Line a 22.5cm/9 inch flan tin (pie pan) with the pastry, then chill. Prick the pastry well and bake blind in a fairly hot oven, 200°C/400°F/Gas 6, for 15 minutes. Leave to cool.

Brush the butter on the pastry base (shell) and cover with the sliced cheese and the olives. Beat together the eggs and cream, and season well (the olives may be a little salty, so it is likely that there will be little need for additional salt). Pour into the pastry case (shell) and sprinkle with the grated cheese. Bake in a fairly hot oven, 190°C/375°F/Gas 5, for 30 minutes. Eat hot.

ONION AND OLIVE QUICHE

Metric/imperial		American
275g/10 oz	prepared shortcrust pastry (basic pie pastry)	about $\frac{3}{4}$ lb
50g/2 oz	butter	¼ cup
2×15ml spoons/ 2 tablespoons	oil	3 tablespoons
675g/1½ lb	onions, sliced	1½ lb
	3 eggs, beaten	
75g/3 oz	Gruyère cheese, grated	¾ cup
3×15ml spoons/ 3 tablespoons	double (heavy) cream	4 tablespoons
	6 black (ripe) olives	

Line a 22.5cm/9 inch flan tin (pie pan) with the pastry, then chill. Prick the pastry well and bake blind in a fairly hot oven, 200°C/400°F/Gas 6, for 15 minutes. Leave to cool.

Heat the butter and oil in a pan and cook the onions over gentle heat for 30 minutes, keeping the pan covered, until they are soft and yellow. Remove from the heat and add the eggs and cheese, then stir in the cream.

Pour the mixture into the pastry case (shell) and arrange the olives at intervals. Bake in a moderate oven, 180°C/350°F/Gas 4, for 30 minutes. Eat hot or cold.

LEEK QUICHE

Metric/imperial		American
275g/10 oz	prepared shortcrust pastry (basic pie pastry)	about ¾ lb
40g/1½ oz	butter	3 tablespoons
900g/2 lb	leeks, sliced into rounds	2 lb
	salt, pepper	
	a pinch of nutmeg	
	3 eggs	
300ml/½ pint	single (light) cream	1¼ cups
75g/3 oz	Gruyère cheese, grated	¾ cup

Line a 22.5cm/9 inch flan tin (pie pan) with the pastry, then chill. Prick the pastry well and bake blind in a fairly hot oven, 200°C/400°F/Gas 6, for 15 minutes. Leave to cool.

Melt the butter in a pan and cook the leeks gently until soft and yellow. Season well with salt, pepper and nutmeg, then put the leeks into the pastry case (shell).

Beat together the eggs and cream, and pour this over the leeks. Sprinkle with the cheese, then bake in a fairly hot oven, 190°C/375°F/Gas 5, for 30 minutes. Eat hot or cold.

CARROT AND CREAM CHEESE QUICHE

Metric/imperial		American
275g/10 oz	prepared cheese pastry	about ¾ lb
	2 eggs	
6×15ml spoons/ 6 tablespoons	single (light) cream	7 tablespoons
450g/1 lb	cooked carrots, puréed	1 lb
225g/8 oz	cream cheese	1 cup
1×15ml spoon/ 1 tablespoon	lemon juice	1 tablespoon
1×5ml spoon/ 1 teaspoon	fresh marjoram **or** thyme	1 tablespoon
25g/1 oz	mixed nuts, chopped	¼ cup
	salt, pepper	
25g/1 oz	Parmesan cheese, grated	¼ cup

Line a 22.5cm/9 inch flan tin (pie pan) with the pastry, then chill. Prick the pastry well and bake blind in a fairly hot oven, 200°C/400°F/Gas 6, for 15 minutes. Leave to cool.

Beat together the eggs and cream, then mix with the carrot purée, cream cheese and lemon juice to make an evenly coloured mixture (this can be done with a blender or food processor). Stir in the marjoram or thyme and the nuts, and season with salt and pepper. Put the mixture into the pastry case (shell), sprinkle with the Parmesan cheese, then bake in a fairly hot oven, 200°C/400°F/Gas 6, for 25 minutes. Eat hot or cold.

Carrot and Cream Cheese Quiche

COURGETTE (ZUCCHINI) QUICHE

Metric/imperial		American
275g/10 oz	prepared shortcrust pastry (basic pie pastry)	about ¾ lb
2×15ml spoons/ 2 tablespoons	oil	3 tablespoons
	1 medium onion, finely chopped	
450g/1 lb	courgettes (zucchini), thinly sliced	1 lb
	salt, pepper	
	3 eggs	
150ml/¼ pint	single (light) cream	⅔ cup
100g/4 oz	Cheddar cheese, grated	1 cup

Line a 22.5cm/9 inch flan tin (pie pan) with the pastry, then chill. Prick the pastry well and bake blind in a fairly hot oven, 200°C/400°F/Gas 6, for 15 minutes. Leave to cool.

Heat the oil in a pan and cook the onion until soft. Add the courgettes (zucchini) and cook over low heat for 15 minutes. Drain the oil from the vegetables. Season the onion and courgettes (zucchini) well with salt and pepper, then arrange in the pastry case (shell).

Beat together the eggs and cream, and pour this over the vegetables, then sprinkle with the cheese. Bake in a fairly hot oven, 200°C/400°F/Gas 6, for 25 minutes. Eat hot or cold.

SAGE AND ONION QUICHE

Metric/imperial		American
275g/10 oz	prepared shortcrust pastry (basic pie pastry)	about ¾ lb
25g/1 oz	butter	2 tablespoons
	2 large onions, finely chopped	
75g/3 oz	Sage Derby (sage **or** herb-flavoured) cheese, crumbled	¾ cup
1×5ml spoon/ 1 teaspoon	fresh sage, chopped	1 teaspoon
	3 eggs	
150ml/¼ pint	single (light) cream	⅔ cup
	salt, pepper	

Line a 22.5cm/9 inch flan tin (pie pan) with the pastry, then chill. Prick the pastry well and bake blind in a fairly hot oven, 200°C/400°F/Gas 6, for 15 minutes. Leave to cool.

Melt the butter in a pan and cook the onions until soft. Cool until lukewarm, then sprinkle on to the base of the pastry case (shell). Sprinkle with the cheese and the sage.

Beat together the eggs and cream, and season well, then pour into the pastry case (shell). Bake in a fairly hot oven, 200°C/400°F/Gas 6, for 30 minutes. Eat hot or cold.

ONION AND APPLE QUICHE

Metric/imperial		American
275g/10 oz	prepared shortcrust pastry (basic pie pastry)	about ¾ lb
1×15ml spoon/ 1 tablespoon	oil	1 tablespoon
25g/1 oz	butter	2 tablespoons
450g/1 lb	onions, thinly sliced	1 lb
	1 clove of garlic, crushed	
225g/8 oz	eating apples, peeled, cored and sliced	½ lb
	2 eggs	
4×15ml spoons/ 4 tablespoons	double (heavy) cream	5 tablespoons
	salt, pepper	
25g/1 oz	Parmesan cheese, grated	¼ cup

Line a 22.5cm/9 inch flan tin (pie pan) with the pastry. Heat the oil and butter in a pan, and cook the onions and garlic until soft. Remove from the heat and stir in the apples. Beat together the eggs and cream, then blend into the onion mixture. Season well with salt and pepper.

Put the mixture into the pastry case (shell) and sprinkle with the cheese. Bake in a fairly hot oven, 200°C/400°F/Gas 6, for 35 minutes. Eat hot.

FENNEL AND CHEESE QUICHE

Metric/imperial		American
275g/10 oz	prepared shortcrust pastry (basic pie pastry)	about ¾ lb
450g/1 lb	fennel root, thinly sliced	1 lb
100g/4 oz	cooked ham, cut into matchstick strips	½ cup
100g/4 oz	Gruyère cheese, cut into matchstick strips	1 cup
	salt, pepper	
	a pinch of mustard powder	
	3 eggs	
300ml/½ pint	single (light) cream	1¼ cups
25g/1 oz	Parmesan cheese, grated	¼ cup

Line a 22.5cm/9 inch flan tin (pie pan) with the pastry, then chill. Prick the pastry well and bake blind in a fairly hot oven, 200°C/400°F/Gas 6, for 15 minutes. Leave to cool.

Boil the fennel in salted water for 10 minutes, then drain well and pat dry with kitchen paper. Mix the ham and Gruyère cheese with the fennel, and season well with the salt, pepper and mustard. Spread in the pastry case (shell).

Beat together the eggs and cream, and pour this over the fennel. Sprinkle with the Parmesan cheese, and bake in a fairly hot oven, 200°C/400°F/Gas 6, for 10 minutes. Reduce the heat to moderate, 180°C/350°F/Gas 4, and bake for a further 25 minutes. Eat hot or cold.

CHEESE QUICHE

Metric/imperial		American
275g/10 oz	prepared shortcrust pastry (basic pie pastry)	about ¾ lb
	2 eggs, beaten	
100g/4 oz	Gruyère cheese, grated	1 cup
	salt, pepper	
	a pinch of ground nutmeg	
150ml/¼ pint	double (heavy) cream	⅔ cup
150ml/¼ pint	milk	⅔ cup

Line a 22.5cm/9 inch flan tin (pie pan) with the pastry, then chill. Prick the pastry well and bake blind in a fairly hot oven, 200°C/400°F/Gas 6, for 15 minutes. Leave to cool.

Mix the eggs with the cheese, season with salt, pepper and nutmeg, and stir in the cream and milk. Pour this into the pastry case (shell) and bake in a moderate oven, 180°C/350°F/Gas 4, for 30 minutes. Eat hot or cold.

CHEESE AND APPLE QUICHE

Metric/imperial		American
275g/10 oz	prepared shortcrust pastry (basic pie pastry)	about ¾ lb
15g/½ oz	butter	1 tablespoon
	1 large onion, thinly sliced	
225g/8 oz	Gouda cheese, grated	2 cups
	1 large cooking apple, peeled, cored and thinly sliced	
	3 eggs	
150ml/¼ pint	single (light) cream	⅔ cup
	salt, pepper	

Line a 22.5cm/9 inch flan tin (pie pan) with the pastry, then chill. Prick the pastry well and bake blind in a fairly hot oven, 200°C/400°F/Gas 6, for 15 minutes. Leave to cool.

Melt the butter in a pan and cook the onion until soft. Sprinkle the cheese over the base of the pastry case (shell). Mix the apple and onion, and spread this over the cheese.

Beat together the eggs and cream, and season well with salt and pepper. Pour into the pastry case (shell) and bake in a fairly hot oven, 190°C/375°F/Gas 5, for 30 minutes. Eat hot or cold.

BRIE QUICHE

Metric/imperial		American
275g/10 oz	prepared shortcrust pastry (basic pie pastry)	about ¾ lb
275g/10 oz	Brie	scant ¾ cup
	1 egg **plus** 1 egg white	
50g/2 oz	Gruyère cheese, grated	½ cup
	salt, pepper	
	a pinch of ground nutmeg	

Line a 22.5cm/9 inch flan tin (pie pan) with the pastry, then chill. Prick the pastry well and bake blind in a fairly hot oven, 200°C/400°F/Gas 6, for 15 minutes. Leave to cool.

Break up the Brie with a fork until it is creamy. Work in the egg, egg white and grated cheese, then season with salt, pepper and nutmeg. Spread in the pastry case (shell), and bake in a moderate oven, 180°C/350°F/Gas 4 for 30 minutes. Eat hot.

STILTON AND WALNUT QUICHE

Metric/imperial		American
275g/10 oz	prepared shortcrust pastry (basic pie pastry)	about ¾ lb
175g/6 oz	cream cheese	¾ cup
100g/4 oz	Stilton cheese	¼ lb
	2 eggs	
150ml/¼ pint	single (light) cream	⅔ cup
	pepper	
75g/3 oz	walnuts, coarsely chopped	¾ cup
	GARNISH	
25g/1 oz	walnuts	¼ cup

Line a 22.5cm/9 inch flan tin (pie pan) with the pastry, then chill. Prick the pastry well and bake blind in a fairly hot oven, 200°C/400°F/Gas 6, for 15 minutes. Leave to cool.

Put the cheeses into a bowl and break them up with a fork, mixing lightly. Beat together the eggs and cream, and work into the cheeses, then season well with pepper. Mix the walnuts with the cheese, and pour into the pastry case (shell). Bake in a fairly hot oven, 200°C/400°F/Gas 6, for 20 minutes. Garnish with the remaining walnuts, and bake for a further 10 minutes. Eat hot.

Note Salt is not necessary for this recipe since the cheese will be salty enough.

33

A FEAST OF FLANS

A flan is slightly easier than a quiche for the inexperienced cook to prepare. The filling is more solid, and is generally bound with a sauce or with eggs, so that the baking temperature and timing are not quite so critical. A flan may be used for making the best of a small quantity of fresh or newly leftover food such as roast meat which may be enlivened with vegetables, herbs and seasonings. While all pastry dishes are best when freshly baked, a flan will suffer less than a quiche if it has to be carried to an outdoor meal, or if pieces are left over, because the filling is less delicate and, therefore, less likely to break up.

A wide variety of ingredients have been combined in the flan fillings in this chapter, but if you particularly dislike or cannot obtain one of the ingredients, it is possible to make substitutions. If, for instance, a green pepper is not available, use mushrooms or tomatoes instead; try varying the herbs according to season; or make a different mixture of shellfish. The important thing is to choose the main ingredient which most appeals to you, to add suitable accompaniments in smaller quantities, to bind the mixture with sauce or eggs, and to add piquancy with cheese, herbs and seasonings.

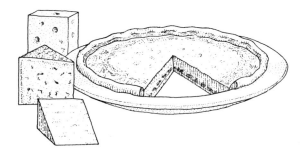

FARMHOUSE CHEESE FLAN

Metric/imperial		American
275g/10 oz	prepared shortcrust pastry (basic pie pastry)	about ¾ lb
25g/1 oz	butter	2 tablespoons
25g/1 oz	plain (all-purpose) flour	¼ cup
300ml/½ pint	milk	1¼ cups
	salt, pepper	
	a pinch of mustard powder	
100g/4 oz	Farmhouse Cheddar cheese, coarsely grated	1 cup
	2 eggs, separated	
1 × 15ml spoon/ 1 tablespoon	chives, finely chopped	1 tablespoon

Line a 22.5cm/9 inch flan tin (pie pan) with the pastry, then chill. Prick the pastry well and bake blind in a fairly hot oven, 200°C/400°F/Gas 6, for 15 minutes. Leave to cool.

Melt the butter in a pan, add the flour and cook for 1 minute. Work in the milk gradually and stir over low heat until smooth and thick. Remove from the heat and season well with salt, pepper and mustard. Stir in the cheese, then beat in the egg yolks. Whisk the egg whites until stiff peaks form, then fold carefully into the cheese.

Pour the mixture into the pastry case (shell), and sprinkle with the chives. Bake in a fairly hot oven, 200°C/400°F/Gas 6, for 30 minutes. Eat hot.

CURRY CHEESE FLAN

Metric/imperial		American
275g/10 oz	prepared shortcrust pastry (basic pie pastry)	about ¾ lb
25g/1 oz	butter	2 tablespoons
25g/1 oz	flour	¼ cup
300ml/½ pint	milk	1¼ cups
100g/4 oz	Cheddar cheese, grated	1 cup
	3 eggs, beaten	
1×5ml spoon/ 1 teaspoon	curry powder	1 teaspoon
	1 clove of garlic, crushed	
	salt, pepper	

Line a 22.5cm/9 inch flan tin (pie pan) with the pastry, then chill. Prick the pastry well and bake blind in a fairly hot oven, 200°C/400°F/Gas 6, for 15 minutes. Leave to cool.

Melt the butter in a pan, add the flour and cook for 1 minute. Work in the milk gradually and stir over low heat until smooth and thick. Remove from the heat, stir in the cheese, eggs, curry powder, garlic, salt and pepper, and mix thoroughly.

Pour the mixture into the pastry case (shell) and bake in a fairly hot oven, 190°C/375°F/Gas 5, for 30 minutes. Eat hot.

ROQUEFORT FLAN

Metric/imperial		American
275g/10 oz	prepared shortcrust pastry (basic pie pastry)	about ¾ lb
25g/1 oz	butter	2 tablespoons
25g/1 oz	flour	¼ cup
300ml/½ pint	milk	1¼ cups
4×15ml spoons/ 4 tablespoons	single (light) cream	5 tablespoons
100g/4 oz	Roquefort cheese, crumbled	1 cup
	salt, pepper	
	a pinch of Cayenne pepper	

Line a 22.5cm/9 inch flan tin (pie pan) with the pastry, then chill. Prick the pastry well and bake blind in a fairly hot oven, 200°C/400°F/Gas 6, for 15 minutes. Leave to cool.

Melt the butter in a pan, add the flour and cook for 1 minute. Work in the milk gradually and stir over low heat until smooth and thick. Remove from the heat, stir in the cream, cheese, salt, pepper and Cayenne pepper, and mix thoroughly.

Pour the mixture into the pastry case (shell) and bake in a fairly hot oven, 200°C/400°F/Gas 6, for 20 minutes. Eat hot.

CHESTNUT AND CHEESE FLAN

Metric/imperial		American
275g/10 oz	prepared cheese pastry	about ¾ lb
225g/8 oz	canned unsweetened chestnut purée	scant 1 cup
50g/2 oz	butter	¼ cup
25g/1 oz	flour	¼ cup
2×5ml spoons/ 2 teaspoons	prepared mustard	2 teaspoons
1×5ml spoon/ 1 teaspoon	mixed fresh herbs, chopped	1 teaspoon
150ml/¼ pint	creamy milk	⅔ cup
	1 egg	
50g/2 oz	Cheddar cheese grated	½ cup
	salt, pepper	
25g/1 oz	fresh breadcrumbs	½ cup
25g/1 oz	Parmesan cheese, grated	¼ cup

Line a 22.5cm/9 inch flan tin (pie pan) with the pastry, then chill. Prick the pastry well and bake blind in a fairly hot oven, 200°C/400°F/Gas 6, for 15 minutes. Leave to cool.

Put the chestnut purée into a pan with the butter, and heat to lukewarm. Sprinkle in the flour, mustard and herbs, and mix well, then cook for 2 minutes. Remove from the heat. Beat together the milk and egg, and stir into the mixture. Return to very low heat and stir for 2 minutes. Remove from the heat again and stir in the Cheddar cheese until melted, then season well with salt and pepper.

Pour the mixture into the pastry case (shell). Mix the breadcrumbs and Parmesan cheese, and sprinkle them over the surface. Bake in a fairly hot oven, 200°C/400°F/Gas 6, for 25 minutes. Eat hot.

EGG AND CHIVE FLAN

Metric/imperial		American
275g/10 oz	prepared shortcrust pastry (basic pie pastry)	about ¾ lb
50g/2 oz	butter	¼ cup
	5 eggs, lightly beaten	
150ml/¼ pint	single (light) cream	⅔ cup
	salt, pepper	
4×15ml spoons/ 4 tablespoons	chopped chives	5 tablespoons

Line a 22.5cm/9 inch flan tin (pie pan) with the pastry, then chill. Prick the pastry well and bake blind in a fairly hot oven, 200°C/400°F/Gas 6, for 20 minutes. Leave to cool.

Melt the butter in a pan and stir in the eggs. Stir over low heat until just beginning to set. Remove from the heat and stir in the cream. Season with salt and pepper and stir in the chives, reserving a small amount for garnish.

Fill the pastry case (shell) with the egg mixture, and sprinkle with the reserved chives. Eat hot.

Variation

Substitute 175g/6 oz peeled prawns (1 US cup shelled shrimp) for the chives, and add to the mixture before filling the pastry case (shell).

Chestnut and Cheese Flan **and** Stilton and Walnut Quiche (page 33)

SURPRISE VEGETABLE FLAN

Metric/imperial		American
275g/10 oz	prepared shortcrust pastry (basic pie pastry)	about ¾ lb
5×15ml spoons/ 5 tablespoons	olive oil	6 tablespoons
450g/1 lb	onions, finely chopped	1 lb
	2 cloves garlic, crushed	
900g/2 lb	ripe tomatoes, roughly chopped	2 lb
	a sprig of thyme	
	1 bay leaf	
	salt, pepper	
	6 eggs	

Line a 22.5cm/9 inch flan tin (pie pan) with the pastry, then chill. Prick the pastry well and bake blind in a fairly hot oven, 200°C/400°F/Gas 6, for 15 minutes. Leave to cool.

Heat half the oil in a pan and simmer the onions and garlic for 30 minutes. In a clean pan, cook the tomatoes with the thyme and bay leaf in the remaining oil until they form a thick purée. Pass the onions and tomatoes through a sieve, and mix together well. Season with salt and pepper.

Spread the cooked vegetables into the pastry case (shell) and bake in a fairly hot oven, 200°C/400°F/Gas 6, for 20 minutes.

Meanwhile, poach the eggs lightly. Arrange them on top of the flan, and serve at once.

LEEK AND TOMATO FLAN

Metric/imperial		American
275g/10 oz	prepared shortcrust pastry (basic pie pastry)	about ¾ lb
25g/1 oz	butter	2 tablespoons
225g/8 oz	leeks, thinly sliced	½ lb
225g/8 oz	cottage cheese	1 cup
	2 eggs	
	salt, pepper	
	4 medium tomatoes, thinly sliced	
1×15ml spoon/ 1 tablespoon	chives, finely chopped	1 tablespoon

Line a 22.5cm/9 inch flan tin (pie pan) with the pastry, then chill. Prick the pastry well and bake blind in a fairly hot oven, 200°C/400°F/Gas 6, for 15 minutes. Leave to cool.

Melt the butter in a pan and cook the leeks very gently for 5 minutes. Drain well and cool to lukewarm. Sieve the cheese, and beat with the eggs and plenty of seasoning.

Put the leeks into the pastry case (shell) and cover with the egg mixture. Arrange the tomatoes on top in a single layer. Bake in a fairly hot oven, 200°C/400°F/Gas 6, for 30 minutes, then sprinkle with the chives. Eat hot or cold.

MUSHROOM FLAN

Metric/imperial		American
275g/10 oz	prepared shortcrust pastry (basic pie pastry)	about ¾ lb
450g/1 lb	button mushrooms, thinly sliced	1 lb
	juice of 1 lemon	
40g/1½ oz	butter	3 tablespoons
15g/½ oz	flour	2 tablespoons
150ml/¼ pint	milk	⅔ cup
	½ bay leaf	
	a sprig of thyme	
150ml/¼ pint	double (heavy) cream	⅔ cup
	2 egg yolks	
	salt, pepper	

Line a 22.5cm/9 inch flan tin (pie pan) with the pastry, then chill. Prick the pastry well and bake blind in a fairly hot oven, 200°C/400°F/Gas 6, for 15 minutes. Leave to cool.

Toss the mushrooms with the lemon juice in a pan over low heat until the juice has been soaked up. Add 25g/1 oz/2 US tablespoons butter, and toss the mushrooms over low heat for 5 minutes.

Melt the remaining butter in a pan, add the flour and cook for 1 minute. Work in the milk gradually and stir over low heat until smooth and thick. Add to the mushrooms with the bay leaf and thyme, and simmer for 5 minutes. Remove the bay leaf and thyme. Remove from the heat and stir in the cream and egg yolks; season well.

Spread the mixture into the pastry case (shell) and bake in a fairly hot oven, 190°C/375°F/Gas 5, for 30 minutes. Eat hot.

ARTICHOKE HEART FLAN

Metric/imperial		American
275g/10 oz	prepared shortcrust pastry (basic pie pastry)	about ¾ lb
350g/12 oz	canned artichoke hearts, drained and halved	12 oz
15g/½ oz	butter	1 tablespoon
15g/½ oz	flour	2 tablespoons
150ml/¼ pint	milk	⅔ cup
	2 eggs	
8×15ml spoons/ 8 tablespoons	single (light) cream	9 tablespoons
50g/2 oz	Parmesan cheese, grated	½ cup
	1 clove of garlic, crushed	
1×15ml spoon/ 1 tablespoon	chopped parsley	1 tablespoon
	salt, pepper	
	a pinch of ground nutmeg	

Line a 22.5cm/9 inch flan tin (pie pan) with the pastry, then chill. Prick the pastry well and bake blind in a fairly hot oven, 200°C/400°F/Gas 6, for 15 minutes. Leave to cool.

Arrange the artichoke hearts in the pastry case (shell). Melt the butter in a pan, add the flour and cook for 1 minute. Work in the milk gradually and stir over low heat until smooth and thick. Remove from the heat, beat together the eggs and cream, and gradually add to the sauce with half the cheese, the garlic, parsley, salt, pepper and nutmeg; mix thoroughly.

Cover the artichoke hearts with this mixture, then sprinkle with the remaining cheese and bake in a fairly hot oven, 190°C/375°F/Gas 5, for 30 minutes. Eat hot.

SPINACH FLAN

Metric/imperial		American
275g/10 oz	prepared shortcrust pastry (basic pie pastry)	about ¾ lb
900g/2 lb	fresh spinach, washed and drained	2 lb
75g/3 oz	butter	6 tablespoons
150ml/¼ pint	double (heavy) cream	⅔ cup
	salt, pepper	
75g/3 oz	Gruyère SWITZERLAND, sliced	¾ cup

Line a 22.5cm/9 inch flan tin (pie pan) with the pastry, then chill. Prick the pastry well and bake blind in a fairly hot oven, 200°C/400°F/Gas 6, for 15 minutes. Leave to cool.

Cook the spinach for 5 minutes in the water which clings to the leaves, then press out all the moisture. Soften the butter slightly, then stir with the cream into the spinach; season well with salt and pepper.

Arrange the spinach in the pastry case (shell) and top with the cheese. Bake in a fairly hot oven, 200°C/400°F/Gas 6, for 20 minutes. Eat very hot.

SHRIMP FLAN

Metric/imperial		American
275g/10 oz	prepared shortcrust pastry (basic pie pastry)	about ¾ lb
225g/8 oz	peeled shrimps	1⅓ cups
15g/½ oz	butter	1 tablespoon
15g/½ oz	flour	2 tablespoons
150ml/¼ pint	milk	⅔ cup
	1 egg	
6×15ml spoons/ 6 tablespoons	single (light) cream	7 tablespoons
50g/2 oz	Cheddar cheese, grated	½ cup
	salt, pepper	

Line a 22.5cm/9 inch flan tin (pie pan) with the pastry, then chill. Prick the pastry well and bake blind in a fairly hot oven, 200°C/400°F/Gas 6, for 15 minutes. Leave to cool.

Arrange the shrimps in the pastry case (shell). Melt the butter in a pan, add the flour and cook for 1 minute. Work in the milk gradually and stir over low heat until smooth and thick. Remove from the heat, beat together the egg and cream, and gradually add to the sauce with the cheese, salt and pepper; mix thoroughly.

Pour this mixture over the shrimps and bake in a fairly hot oven, 190°C/375°F/Gas 5, for 30 minutes. Eat hot.

Spinach Flan

KIPPER SOUFFLÉ FLAN

Metric/imperial		American
275g/10 oz	prepared shortcrust pastry (basic pie pastry)	about ¾ lb
175g/6 oz	kipper fillets	⅓ lb
15g/½ oz	butter	1 tablespoon
15g/½ oz	flour	2 tablespoons
150ml/¼ pint	milk	⅔ cup
	salt, pepper	
	2 eggs, separated	
15g/½ oz	Parmesan cheese, grated	1 tablespoon

Line a 22.5cm/9 inch flan tin (pie pan) with the pastry, then chill. Prick the pastry well and bake blind in a fairly hot oven, 200°C/400°F/Gas 6, for 15 minutes. Leave to cool.

Meanwhile, poach the kipper fillets in a little water until tender, then remove the skin and flake the fish.

Melt the butter in a pan, add the flour and cook for 1 minute. Work in the milk gradually and stir over low heat until smooth and thick. Remove from the heat and cool until lukewarm. Stir in the fish, salt, pepper and egg yolks. Whisk the egg whites until soft peaks form, then fold carefully into the fish mixture.

Spoon the mixture into the pastry case (shell) and sprinkle with the cheese. Bake in a fairly hot oven, 200°C/400°F/Gas 6, for 30 minutes until the filling is risen and golden. Eat at once.

KIPPER AND EGG FLAN

Metric/imperial		American
275g/10 oz	prepared shortcrust pastry (basic pie pastry)	about ¾ lb
175g/6 oz	kipper fillets	⅓ lb
	2 hard-boiled eggs, chopped	
225g/8 oz	cottage cheese	1 cup
	grated rind and juice of 1 lemon	
1×15ml spoon/ 1 tablespoon	chopped parsley	1 tablespoon
	salt, pepper	
	2 eggs, beaten	

Line a 22.5cm/9 inch flan tin (pie pan) with the pastry, then chill. Prick the pastry well and bake blind in a fairly hot oven, 200°C/400°F/Gas 6, for 15 minutes. Leave to cool.

Meanwhile, poach the kipper fillets in a little water until tender, then remove the skin and flake the fish. Mix with the hard-boiled eggs and cottage cheese, then add the lemon rind and juice, the parsley, seasoning and beaten eggs.

Spread the mixture in the pastry case (shell) and bake in a fairly hot oven, 190°C/375°F/Gas 5, for 30 minutes. Eat hot.

ANCHOVY HERB FLAN

Metric/imperial		American
275g/10 oz	prepared shortcrust pastry (basic pie pastry)	about ¾ lb
	20 anchovy fillets, drained	
1×15ml spoon/ 1 tablespoon	olive oil	1 tablespoon
450g/1 lb	ripe tomatoes, thinly sliced	1 lb
	salt, pepper	
1×15ml spoon/ 1 tablespoon	chopped basil **or** chives	1 tablespoon

Line a 22.5cm/9 inch flan tin (pie pan) with the pastry. Put the anchovy fillets into the oil. Arrange the tomato slices in the pastry case (shell), season well with salt and pepper, and sprinkle with a little of the oil used for the anchovy fillets. Arrange the anchovy fillets in lines across the tomatoes. Sprinkle with the basil or chives, and then sprinkle with the oil. Bake in a fairly hot oven, 200°C/400°F/Gas 6, for 30 minutes. Eat hot or cold.

DUTCH FLAN

Metric/imperial		American
275g/10 oz	prepared puff pastry	about ¾ lb
25g/1 oz	butter	2 tablespoons
	1 large onion, finely chopped	
225g/8 oz	canned tomatoes	1 cup
1×2.5ml spoon/ ½ teaspoon	marjoram	½ teaspoon
	salt, pepper	
175g/6 oz	Gouda cheese, grated	1½ cups
50g/2 oz	anchovy fillets, drained	2 oz
	black (ripe) olives	

Line a 22.5cm/9 inch flan tin (pie pan) with the pastry. Melt the butter in a pan and cook the onion until soft. Add the tomatoes, marjoram, salt and pepper, and simmer for 10 minutes. Spread on the pastry base (shell). Sprinkle with the cheese, and arrange a lattice of anchovy fillets on top. Garnish with the olives. Bake in a hot oven, 220°C/425°F/Gas 7, for 30 minutes. Eat hot.

PISSALADIÈRE

Metric/imperial		American
275g/10 oz	prepared shortcrust pastry (basic pie pastry)	about ¾ lb
7×15ml spoons/ 7 tablespoons	olive oil	8 tablespoons
900g/2 lb	onions, finely chopped	2 lb
	3 cloves garlic, crushed	
	6 large tomatoes, skinned and roughly chopped	
	salt, pepper	
50g/2 oz	anchovy fillets, drained	2 oz
	10 black (ripe) olives, stoned (pitted) and halved	

Line a 22.5cm/9 inch flan tin (pie pan) with the pastry, then chill. Prick the pastry well and bake blind in a fairly hot oven, 200°C/400°F/Gas 6, for 15 minutes. Leave to cool.

Heat the oil in a pan and cook the onions and garlic for about 30 minutes until very soft but not browned. Add the tomatoes and cook for a further 10 minutes. Season well with salt and pepper.

Spread the onion mixture in the pastry case (shell). Arrange the anchovy fillets in a lattice pattern on top, and garnish with the olives. Sprinkle with a little extra oil. Bake in a fairly hot oven, 200°C/400°F/Gas 6, for 25 minutes. Eat hot or cold.

SMOKED SALMON FLAN

Metric/imperial		American
275g/10 oz	prepared shortcrust pastry (basic pie pastry)	about ¾ lb
15g/½ oz	flour	2 tablespoons
150ml/¼ pint	milk	⅔ cup
6×15ml spoons/ 6 tablespoons	single (light) cream	7 tablespoons
15g/½ oz	butter, cut into small pieces	1 tablespoon
	juice of 1 lemon	
	2 eggs, beaten	
	salt, pepper	
225g/8 oz	smoked salmon, cut into thin strips	½ lb

Line a 22.5cm/9 inch flan tin (pie pan) with the pastry, then chill. Prick the pastry well and bake blind in a fairly hot oven, 200°C/400°F/Gas 6, for 15 minutes. Leave to cool.

Mix the flour with a little of the milk, and then gradually work in the rest of the milk and the cream. Heat gently, stirring well, until the mixture is creamy. Remove from the heat and add the butter and lemon juice. Beat in the eggs, season well with salt and pepper, then add half the smoked salmon.

Spread the mixture in the pastry case (shell) and bake in a fairly hot oven, 190°C/375°F/Gas 5, for 30 minutes. Garnish with the remaining salmon pieces. Eat warm.

Honey Apple Tart (page 62) **and** Smoked Salmon Flan

FISHERMAN'S FLAN

Metric/imperial		American
275g/10 oz	prepared shortcrust pastry (basic pie pastry)	about ¾ lb
15g/½ oz	butter	1 tablespoon
15g/½ oz	flour	2 tablespoons
150ml/¼ pint	dry (hard) cider	⅔ cup
	1 egg	
4×15ml spoons/ 4 tablespoons	single (light) cream	5 tablespoons
225g/8 oz	cooked smoked haddock (finnan haddie), flaked	1 cup
	2 hard-boiled eggs, finely chopped	
100g/4 oz	cooked peas	¾ cup
	salt, pepper	
25g/1 oz	Parmesan cheese, grated	¼ cup

Line a 22.5cm/9 inch flan tin (pie pan) with the pastry, then chill. Prick the pastry well and bake blind in a fairly hot oven, 200°C/400°F/Gas 6, for 15 minutes. Leave to cool.

Melt the butter in a pan, add the flour and cook for 1 minute. Gradually add the cider, and stir over low heat for 5 minutes until creamy. Remove from the heat, beat together the egg and cream, and gradually add to the sauce with the haddock, eggs, peas, salt and pepper; mix thoroughly.

Spread the mixture in the pastry case (shell) and sprinkle with the grated cheese. Bake in a fairly hot oven, 190°C/375°F/Gas 5, for 30 minutes. Eat hot.

SMOKED HADDOCK (FINNAN HADDIE) AND CHEESE FLAN

Metric/imperial		American
275g/10 oz	prepared shortcrust pastry (basic pie pastry)	about ¾ lb
15g/½ oz	butter	1 tablespoon
15g/½ oz	flour	2 tablespoons
150ml/¼ pint	milk	⅔ cup
	1 egg	
150ml/¼ pint	single (light) cream	⅔ cup
100g/4 oz	cooked smoked haddock (finnan haddie), flaked	½ cup
100g/4 oz	Cheddar cheese, grated	1 cup
1×15ml spoon/ 1 tablespoon	chopped parsley	1 tablespoon
	salt, pepper	

Line a 22.5cm/9 inch flan tin (pie pan) with the pastry, then chill. Prick the pastry well and bake blind in a fairly hot oven, 200°C/400°F/Gas 6, for 15 minutes. Leave to cool.

Melt the butter in a pan, add the flour and cook for 1 minute. Work in the milk gradually, and stir over low heat until smooth and thick. Remove from the heat, beat together the egg and cream, and gradually add to the sauce with the haddock, cheese, parsley, salt and pepper; mix thoroughly.

Spread the mixture in the pastry case (shell) and bake in a fairly hot oven, 190°C/375°F/Gas 5, for 30 minutes. Eat hot.

BEEF AND MUSTARD FLAN

Metric/imperial		American
275g/10 oz	prepared shortcrust pastry (basic pie pastry)	about ¾ lb
25g/1 oz	butter	2 tablespoons
	1 small onion, finely chopped	
450g/1 lb	raw minced (ground) beef	2 cups
25g/1 oz	flour	¼ cup
450ml/¾ pint	beef stock	2 cups
1×15ml spoon/ 1 tablespoon	prepared mustard	1 tablespoon
	salt, pepper	
	4 large tomatoes, sliced	

Line a 22.5cm/9 inch flan tin (pie pan) with the pastry, then chill. Prick the pastry well and bake blind in a fairly hot oven, 200°C/400°F/Gas 6, for 15 minutes. Leave to cool.

Melt the butter in a pan and cook the onion until soft. In another pan, cook the minced (ground) beef over low heat until the meat is coloured light brown. Drain off the surplus fat. Work the flour into the onion and cook for 1 minute. Add the stock, and stir over low heat until smooth. Stir in the mustard, and season with salt and pepper. Add the beef, and mix well.

Spread the mixture in the pastry case (shell) and arrange the tomatoes in a layer on top. Bake in a fairly hot oven, 200°C/ 400°F/Gas 6, for 25 minutes. Eat hot.

CURRIED LAMB FLAN

Metric/imperial		American
275g/10 oz	prepared shortcrust pastry (basic pie pastry)	about ¾ lb
15g/½ oz	butter	1 tablespoon
	1 small onion, finely chopped	
15g/⅓ oz	flour	2 tablespoons
300ml/½ pint	beef stock	1¼ cups
1×5ml spoon/ 1 teaspoon	curry powder	1 teaspoon
	salt, pepper	
225g/8 oz	cooked lamb, diced	1 cup
	1 small apple, peeled, cored and diced	
25g/1 oz	desiccated (shredded) coconut	⅓ cup
25g/1 oz	sultanas (golden raisins)	2 tablespoons

Line a 22.5cm/9 inch flan tin (pie pan) with the pastry, then chill. Prick the pastry well and bake blind in a fairly hot oven, 200°C/400°F/Gas 6, for 15 minutes. Leave to cool.

Melt the butter in a pan and cook the onion until soft. Work in the flour, and stir over low heat for 1 minute. Add the stock and curry powder, and stir over low heat until the mixture thickens and boils. Season to taste with salt and pepper. Stir in the meat, apple, coconut and sultanas (golden raisins). Heat through, then leave to cool so that the flavours blend.

Spread the mixture in the pastry case (shell) and bake in a fairly hot oven, 190°C/375°F/Gas 5, for 30 minutes. Eat hot or cold.

Sausage, Mushroom and Bacon Flan

Metric/imperial		American
275g/10 oz	prepared shortcrust pastry (basic pie pastry)	about ¾ lb
25g/1 oz	butter	2 tablespoons
	1 small onion, finely chopped	
	2 small leeks, finely chopped	
	3 back bacon rashers, (Canadian bacon slices) rinds removed and coarsely chopped	
100g/4 oz	mushrooms, sliced	1 cup
450g/1 lb	pork sausage-meat	1 lb
1×5ml spoon/ 1 teaspoon	prepared mustard	1 teaspoon
1×15ml spoon/ 1 tablespoon	chopped parsley	1 tablespoon
	salt, pepper	
	2 eggs, beaten	

Line a 22.5cm/9 inch flan tin (pie pan) with the pastry, then chill. Prick the pastry well and bake blind in a fairly hot oven, 200°C/400°F/Gas 6, for 15 minutes. Leave to cool.

Melt the butter in a pan and cook the onion and leeks until soft. Add the bacon and mushrooms, and continue cooking until the onion is golden. Stir in the sausage-meat, and cook for 15 minutes, stirring frequently. Drain off the excess fat, then season with mustard, parsley, salt and pepper.

Spread the mixture in the pastry case (shell) and pour over the eggs. Bake in a fairly hot oven, 190°C/375°F/Gas 5, for 30 minutes. Eat hot or cold.

Pork and Apple Flan

Metric/imperial		American
275g/10 oz	prepared shortcrust pastry (basic pie pastry)	about ¾ lb
450g/1 lb	lean pork, finely chopped	1 lb
100g/4 oz	bacon, rinds removed and finely chopped	½ cup
	1 small onion, finely chopped	
1×15ml spoon/ 1 tablespoon	fresh sage, chopped	1 tablespoon
450ml/¾ pint	dry white wine	2 cups
25g/1 oz	butter	2 tablespoons
25g/1 oz	flour	¼ cup
	salt, pepper	
	a pinch of ground nutmeg	
	4 eating apples, peeled, cored and finely chopped	

Line a 22.5cm/9 inch flan tin (pie pan) with the pastry, then chill. Prick the pastry well and bake blind in a fairly hot oven, 200°C/400°F/Gas 6, for 15 minutes. Leave to cool.

Put the pork, bacon and onion into a pan with the sage and wine, and simmer until tender. Drain well, reserving the liquid.

Melt the butter in a pan, add the flour and cook for 1 minute. Make up the reserved cooking liquid to 450ml/¾ pint/2 US cups with water, and work into the butter and flour. Stir over low heat until smooth and thick. Remove from the heat and stir in the pork mixture, then season well with salt, pepper and nutmeg. Add the chopped apples, and mix thoroughly.

Spread the mixture in the pastry case (shell) and bake in a fairly hot oven, 200°C/400°F/Gas 6, for 25 minutes. Eat hot or cold.

SPRING VEGETABLE FLAN

Metric/imperial		American
275g/10 oz	prepared shortcrust pastry (basic pie pastry)	about ¾ lb
50g/2 oz	butter	¼ cup
100g/4 oz	small carrots, sliced	1 cup
100g/4 oz	French (green) beans, sliced	½ cup
100g/4 oz	tomatoes, roughly chopped	½ cup
	1 small onion, finely chopped	
	1 small green pepper, de-seeded and finely chopped	
100g/4 oz	back bacon, (Canadian bacon), roughly chopped	½ cup
	salt, pepper	
225g/8 oz	Gouda cheese, grated	2 cups

Line a 22.5cm/9 inch flan tin (pie pan) with the pastry. Melt the butter in a pan and cook the vegetables and bacon until just tender. Season well with salt and pepper, and leave until cold.

Pack the mixture into the pastry case, (shell) then cover the top of the flan with foil and bake in a fairly hot oven, 200°C/400°F/Gas 6, for 45 minutes. Remove the foil. Sprinkle the cheese thickly over the vegetables, and return to the oven for a further 15 minutes until the cheese is golden-brown and melted. Eat hot.

SOUFFLÉ FLAN

Metric/imperial		American
275g/10 oz	prepared shortcrust pastry (basic pie pastry)	about ¾ lb
25g/1 oz	flour	¼ cup
300ml/½ pint	milk	1¼ cups
100g/4 oz	butter, cut into small pieces	½ cup
	2 eggs, separated	
50g/2 oz	Cheddar cheese, grated	½ cup
175g/6 oz	Gruyère cheese, thinly sliced	1½ cups
175g/6 oz	slice gammon (ham), cubed	¾ cup
	salt, pepper	
	a pinch of ground nutmeg	

Line a 22.5cm/9 inch flan tin (pie pan) with the pastry, then chill. Prick the pastry well and bake blind in a fairly hot oven, 200°C/400°F/Gas 6, for 15 minutes. Leave to cool.

Mix the flour with a little of the milk, and gradually work in the remaining milk. Heat gently, stirring well, until thick and creamy. Remove from the heat and stir in the butter, egg yolks and grated cheese.

Arrange the cheese slices and gammon (ham) in the pastry case (shell). Whisk the egg whites to soft peaks and fold into the cheese sauce. Season well with salt, pepper and nutmeg, and pour into the pastry case (shell). Bake in a moderate oven 180°C/350°F/Gas 4, for 40 minutes. Eat hot.

CHICKEN AND MUSHROOM FLAN

Metric/imperial		American
275g/10 oz	prepared shortcrust pastry (basic pie pastry)	about ¾ lb
25g/1 oz	butter	2 tablespoons
25g/1 oz	flour	¼ cup
300ml/½ pint	milk	1¼ cups
225g/8 oz	cooked chicken, diced	1 cup
50g/2 oz	button mushrooms, thinly sliced	½ cup
	salt, pepper	
4×15ml spoons/ 4 tablespoons	single (light) cream	5 tablespoons

Line a 22.5cm/9 inch flan tin (pie pan) with the pastry, then chill. Prick the pastry well and bake blind in a fairly hot oven, 200°C/400°F/Gas 6, for 15 minutes. Leave to cool.

Melt the butter in a pan, add the flour and cook for 1 minute. Work in the milk gradually and stir over low heat until smooth and thick. Remove from the heat and mix together with the chicken and mushrooms. Season well and stir in the cream.

Spread the mixture in the pastry case (shell) and bake in a fairly hot oven, 190°C/375°F/Gas 5, for 30 minutes. Eat hot or cold.

SPICED TURKEY FLAN

Metric/imperial		American
275g/10 oz	prepared shortcrust pastry (basic pie pastry)	about ¾ lb
25g/1 oz	butter	2 tablespoons
	1 small onion, finely chopped	
15g/½ oz	flour	2 tablespoons
1×15ml spoon/ 1 tablespoon	curry powder	1 tablespoon
300ml/½ pint	turkey stock (see **Note**)	1¼ cups
	2 eggs	
4×15ml spoons/ 4 tablespoons	single (light) cream	5 tablespoons
350g/12 oz	cooked turkey, diced	1½ cups
2×15ml spoons/ 2 tablespoons	sweet chutney, finely chopped	3 tablespoons
1×15ml spoon/ 1 tablespoon	lemon juice	1 tablespoon

Line a 22.5cm/9 inch flan tin (pie pan) with the pastry, then chill. Prick the pastry well and bake blind in a fairly hot oven, 200°C/400°F/Gas 6, for 15 minutes. Leave to cool.

Melt the butter in a pan, and cook the onion until soft. Work in the flour and curry powder, and cook for 1 minute. Add the stock gradually and stir over gentle heat for 10 minutes until smooth and thick. Remove from the heat, beat together the eggs and cream, and gradually add to the sauce with the turkey, chutney and lemon juice; mix thoroughly.

Spread the mixture in the pastry case (shell) and bake in a fairly hot oven, 190°C/375°F/Gas 5, for 30 minutes. Eat hot or cold.

Note The turkey stock can be prepared from the liquid used to cook the turkey. Chicken stock can be substituted, if liked.

SWEET ENDINGS

Pastry is always a popular ending for a meal, and a sweet tart can delight the eye as well as the taste-buds. Plain shortcrust (basic pie pastry) or puff pastry may be used, but sweet shortcrust (sweet pie) pastry is particularly good with fruit fillings and has a delicious biscuit (cookie) texture. Sweet shortcrust (sweet pie) pastry can be a little difficult to handle, and it is best to use a flan tin (pie pan) with a removable base so that the cooked tart does not have to be handled.

Some tarts do not need baking after filling, and it is then best to assemble them as late as possible before serving them. A pastry case may be baked ahead and stored in a tin or in the freezer, ready to be filled quickly with confectioner's custard, fruit and a finishing glaze, so that it tastes really fresh and appetizing.

Sweet tarts are, of course, delicious on their own, but pouring cream, whipped cream or vanilla ice cream may be served as accompaniments.

CHOCOLATE TART

Metric/imperial		American
225g/8 oz	prepared sweet shortcrust pastry (sweet pie pastry)	½ lb
75g/3 oz	plain (semi-sweet) chocolate	3 squares
2 × 5ml spoons/ 2 teaspoons	coffee essence (strong black coffee)	2 teaspoons
75g/3 oz	unsalted butter	6 tablespoons
	3 eggs, separated	
75g/3 oz	granulated sugar	6 tablespoons
75g/3 oz	flour	¾ cup

Line a 20cm/8 inch flan tin (pie pan) with the pastry, then chill. Prick the pastry well and bake blind in a fairly hot oven, 200°C/400°F/Gas 6, for 15 minutes. Leave to cool.

Put the chocolate into a bowl with the coffee essence, and heat over a pan of hot water until melted. Remove from the heat and beat in the butter and egg yolks with the sugar and flour. Whisk the egg whites until stiff peaks form, and fold into the chocolate mixture.

Fill the pastry case (shell) with the chocolate mixture, and bake in a moderate oven, 180°C/350°F/Gas 4, for 25 minutes. Eat hot or cold with sweetened whipped cream.

BUTTERSCOTCH FLAN

Metric/imperial		American
225g/8 oz	prepared wholemeal shortcrust pastry (wholewheat pie pastry)	½ lb
100g/4 oz	dark soft brown sugar	½ cup
50g/2 oz	butter	¼ cup
	1 egg, separated	
100g/4 oz	cornflour (cornstarch)	1 cup
300ml/½ pint	milk	1¼ cups
	a pinch of salt	
50g/2 oz	Demerara (brown) sugar	¼ cup

Line a 17.5cm/7 inch flan tin (pie pan) with the pastry, then chill. Prick the pastry well and bake blind in a fairly hot oven, 200°C/400°F/Gas 6, for 15 minutes. Leave to cool.

Put the dark soft brown sugar and butter into a bowl over a pan of hot water, and heat until melted, then beat in the egg yolk. Mix the cornflour (cornstarch) with 1×15ml spoon/1 tablespoon water, and add to the bowl. Work in the milk and salt, and cook until the mixture is smooth and thick. Cool to lukewarm.

Spread the mixture in the pastry case (shell). Whisk the egg white until stiff peaks form, then fold in the Demerara (brown) sugar. Pile the meringue on top of the filling, and bake in a warm oven, 160°C/325°F/Gas 3, for 15 minutes. Eat hot or cold.

COTTAGE CHEESE AND RAISIN TART

Metric/imperial		American
225g/8 oz	prepared sweet shortcrust pastry (sweet pie pastry)	½ lb
450g/1 lb	cottage cheese, sieved	2 cups
	3 eggs, separated	
75g/3 oz	granulated sugar	6 tablespoons
75g/3 oz	seedless raisins	½ cup
150ml/¼ pint	double (heavy) cream	⅔ cup
	a pinch of ground cinnamon	

Line a 20cm/8 inch flan tin (pie pan) with the pastry, then chill. Prick the pastry well and bake blind in a fairly hot oven, 200°C/400°F/Gas 6, for 15 minutes.

Mix the cottage cheese with the egg yolks, sugar, raisins and cream. Whisk the egg whites until stiff peaks form, and fold into the mixture.

Pile the mixture into the pastry case (shell) and dust with cinnamon. Bake in a moderate oven, 180°C/350°F/Gas 4, for 30 minutes. Leave the tart in the oven until cold.

Cottage Cheese and Raisin Tart **and** Butterscotch Flan

DUKE OF CAMBRIDGE TART

Metric/imperial		American
225g/8 oz	prepared sweet shortcrust pastry (sweet pie pastry)	½ lb
75g/3 oz	chunky orange marmalade	⅓ cup
	2 egg yolks	
75g/3 oz	butter	6 tablespoons
75g/3 oz	granulated sugar	6 tablespoons

Line a 20cm/8 inch flan tin (pie pan) with the pastry, then chill. Prick the pastry well and bake blind in a fairly hot oven, 200°C/400°F/Gas 6, for 15 minutes. Leave to cool.

Spread the marmalade in the pastry case (shell). Put the egg yolks, butter and sugar into a small pan and cook gently over low heat until the mixture bubbles. Pour this over the marmalade and bake in a warm oven, 160°C/325°F/Gas 3, for 20 minutes. Serve cold with whipped cream.

TREACLE CREAM TART

Metric/imperial		American
225g/8 oz	prepared shortcrust pastry (basic pie pastry)	½ lb
225g/8 oz	golden (light corn) syrup	⅔ cup
50g/2 oz	butter	¼ cup
	1 egg	
5×15ml spoons 5 tablespoons	single (light) cream	6 tablespoons
1×2.5ml spoon/ ½ teaspoon	grated lemon rind	½ teaspoon

Line a 20cm/8 inch flan tin (pie pan) with the pastry. Warm the syrup with the butter until the butter has melted. Beat together the egg and cream, and pour in the syrup mixture, mixing well. Add the lemon rind, then pour into the pastry case (shell). Bake in a fairly hot oven, 200°C/400°F/Gas 6, for 30 minutes. Eat hot or cold.

CUSTARD TARTS

Metric/imperial		American
275g/10 oz	prepared shortcrust pastry (basic pie pastry)	about ¾ lb
300ml/½ pint	milk	1¼ cups
	2 eggs	
15g/½ oz	sugar	1 tablespoon
	ground nutmeg	

Line 12 deep patty tins (pans) with the pastry, pressing it very firmly against the bases and edges. Place a baking sheet in a fairly hot oven, 190°C/375°F/Gas 5. Heat the milk to just under boiling point. Beat together the eggs and sugar, and pour in the hot milk, stirring well. Strain into a jug.

Fill each pastry case (shell) two-thirds full with the custard, and sprinkle the nutmeg on top. Place on the hot baking sheet and bake in a fairly hot oven, 190°C/375°F/Gas 5, for 15 minutes. Reduce the heat to moderate, 180°C/350°F/Gas 4, and bake for a further 20 minutes. Eat hot or cold.

LEMON TART

Metric/imperial		American
225g/8 oz	prepared sweet shortcrust pastry (sweet pie pastry)	½ lb
	2 eggs	
200g/7 oz	caster sugar	¾ cup + 2 tablespoons
75g/3 oz	butter, softened	6 tablespoons
	rind and juice of 2 lemons	

Line a 20cm/8 inch flan tin (pie pan) with the pastry. Beat together the eggs and sugar, and work in the butter. Work the lemon rind and juice into the egg mixture, then pour this into the pastry case (shell). Bake in a fairly hot oven, 190°C/375°F/ Gas 5, for 35 minutes. Eat cold.

REDCURRANT TART

Metric/imperial		American
225g/8 oz	prepared sweet shortcrust pastry (sweet pie pastry)	½ lb
450g/1 lb	redcurrants	1 lb
6 × 15ml spoons/ 6 tablespoons	water	7 tablespoons
175g/6 oz	granulated sugar	¾ cup

Line a 20cm/8 inch flan tin (pie pan) with the pastry, then chill. Prick the pastry well and bake blind in a fairly hot oven, 200°C/400°F/Gas 6, for 15 minutes. Leave to cool.

Cook half the currants in a pan with the water for 10 minutes, then pass through a sieve. Return the purée to the pan and stir in the sugar until dissolved. Bring to the boil, then simmer for 5 minutes. Leave until lukewarm, then stir in the remaining redcurrants. Spoon the purée into the pastry case (shell), and serve at once.

ORANGE CREAM TART

Metric/imperial		American
225g/8 oz	prepared sweet shortcrust pastry (sweet pie pastry)	½ lb
	2 egg yolks	
50g/2 oz	caster sugar	¼ cup
25g/1 oz	flour	¼ cup
300ml/½ pint	milk	1¼ cups
	grated rind of 1 orange	
	2 oranges, peeled and pith removed	
2×15ml spoons/ 2 tablespoons	orange marmalade	3 tablespoons
1×5ml spoon/ 1 teaspoon	orange liqueur	1 teaspoon

Line a 20cm/8 inch flan tin (pie pan) with the pastry. Prick the pastry well and bake blind in a fairly hot oven, 200°C/400°F/Gas 6, for 15 minutes. Leave to cool.

Mix together the egg yolks, sugar and flour until smooth. Heat the milk to just under boiling point, then pour on to the egg yolks, mix well and return to the saucepan. Add the orange rind, and stir the mixture over low heat for 3 minutes. Leave to cool.

Pour the custard into the pastry case (shell). Cut the oranges crossways into thin slices and arrange on top of the custard. Heat the marmalade until just liquid, and stir in the orange liqueur. Brush this glaze over the orange slices. Eat freshly made.

PUMPKIN PIE

Metric/imperial		American
225g/8 oz	prepared sweet shortcrust pastry (sweet pie pastry)	½ lb
450g/1 lb	pumpkin, de-seeded, peeled and cut into pieces	1 lb
	1 egg, separated	
75g/3 oz	light soft brown sugar	6 tablespoons
½×2.5ml spoon/ ¼ teaspoon	ground ginger	¼ teaspoon
½×2.5ml spoon/ ¼ teaspoon	ground cinnamon	¼ teaspoon
200ml/6 fl oz	milk	¾ cup
50g/2 oz	seedless raisins	⅓ cup
	a few drops vanilla essence (extract)	
	grated rind and juice of ½ lemon	
	a pinch of salt	

Line a 20cm/8 inch flan tin (pie pan) with the pastry. Steam the pumpkin for 35–40 minutes or until tender, then drain. Mix with the egg yolk, sugar, spices, milk, raisins, vanilla essence (extract), lemon rind and juice and the salt. Whisk the egg white until soft peaks form, then fold into the mixture.

Fill the pastry case (shell) with the mixture, and bake in a fairly hot oven, 200°C/400°F/Gas 6, for 10 minutes, then reduce the heat and bake at 190°C/375°F/Gas 5, for 30 minutes. Eat hot or cold.

Pumpkin Pie

BLACKCURRANT TART

Metric/imperial		American
225g/8 oz	prepared sweet shortcrust pastry (sweet pie pastry)	½ lb
350g/12 oz	blackcurrants	¾ lb
75g/3 oz	caster sugar	6 tablespoons
1×2.5ml spoon/ ½ teaspoon	ground cinnamon	½ teaspoon
	redcurrant glaze (page 14)	

Line a 20cm/8 inch flan tin (pie pan) with the pastry. Arrange the blackcurrants in the pastry case (shell). Mix together the caster sugar and cinnamon, and sprinkle this over the fruit. Bake in a fairly hot oven, 200°C/400°F/Gas 6, for 30 minutes. As soon as the tart is cooked, brush the warm glaze over the fruit. Eat hot or cold.

APRICOT TART

Metric/imperial		American
225g/8 oz	prepared sweet shortcrust pastry (sweet pie pastry)	½ lb
175g/6 oz	caster sugar	¾ cup
675g/1½ lb	ripe fresh apricots, halved and stoned (pitted)	1½ lb

Line a 20cm/8 inch flan tin (pie pan) with the pastry, and sprinkle the base with 50g/2 oz/¼ US cup sugar. Arrange the apricot halves close together on the pastry base (shell), cut side up. Sprinkle thickly with the remaining sugar. Bake in a hot oven, 220°C/425°F/Gas 7, for 30 minutes. Eat hot or cold.

DANISH CHERRY ALMOND TART

Metric/imperial		American
225g/8 oz	prepared sweet shortcrust pastry (sweet pie pastry)	½ lb
225g/8 oz	black (bing) cherries, stoned (pitted)	½ lb
100g/4 oz	ground almonds	1 cup
175g/6 oz	icing (confectioner's) sugar	1½ cups
	2 eggs	

Line a 20cm/8 inch flan tin (pie pan) with the pastry. Arrange the cherries in the pastry case (shell). Stir together the ground almonds and icing sugar, and work in the eggs to make a soft paste. Spread this over the cherries. Bake in a fairly hot oven, 200°C/400°F/Gas 6, for 30 minutes. Eat hot or cold.

RASPBERRY CREAM TART

Metric/imperial		American
225g/8 oz	prepared sweet shortcrust pastry (sweet pie pastry)	½ lb
225g/8 oz	raspberries	½ lb
50g/2 oz	caster sugar	¼ cup
75g/3 oz	cream cheese	6 tablespoons
150ml/¼ pint	double (heavy) cream	⅔ cup
2×5ml spoons/ 2 teaspoons	clear honey	2 teaspoons
25g/1 oz	muesli (granola)	2 tablespoons
25g/1 oz	Demerara (brown) sugar	2 tablespoons

Line a 20cm/8 inch flan tin (pie pan) with the pastry, then chill. Prick the pastry well and bake blind in a fairly hot oven, 200°C/400°F/Gas 6, for 15 minutes. Leave to cool.

Fill the pastry case (shell) with the raspberries, and sprinkle with the caster sugar. Mash the cream cheese with a fork, then beat with a wooden spoon until soft, gradually working in the cream and honey. Pile the cream mixture on to the raspberries. Mix together the muesli (granola) and Demerara (brown) sugar, and sprinkle on top. Serve chilled.

GOOSEBERRY AMBER TART

Metric/imperial		American
225g/8 oz	prepared shortcrust pastry (basic pie pastry)	½ lb
675g/1½ lb	gooseberries	1½ lb
150ml/¼ pint	water	⅔ cup
100g/4 oz	granulated sugar	½ cup
25g/1 oz	butter	2 tablespoons
	2 eggs, separated	
100g/4 oz	caster sugar	½ cup

Line a 20cm/8 inch flan tin (pie pan) with the pastry. Cook the gooseberries in a pan with the water until soft. Add the sugar and stir until dissolved. Continue simmering until the fruit is very soft. Pass through a sieve and cool the purée until lukewarm. Beat in the butter and egg yolks, then pour into the pastry case (shell). Bake in a fairly hot oven, 190°C/375°F/Gas 5, for 35 minutes. Whisk the egg whites until stiff peaks form, and fold in the caster sugar. Spread over the tart, and return to the oven for 10 minutes. Eat hot or cold.

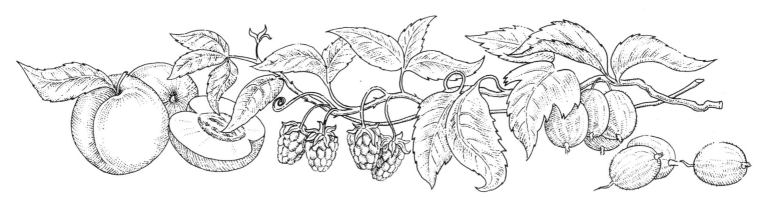

FRENCH GRAPE TART

Metric/imperial		American
225g/8 oz	prepared sweet shortcrust pastry (sweet pie pastry)	½ lb
1×15ml spoon/ 1 tablespoon	orange liqueur	1 tablespoon
300ml/½ pint	confectioner's custard (page 14)	1¼ cups
350g/12 oz	black (purple) grapes, pips removed and halved	¾ lb
	apricot glaze (page 14)	

Line a 20cm/8 inch flan tin (pie pan) with the pastry. Prick the pastry well and bake blind in a fairly hot oven, 200°C/400°F/Gas 6, for 15 minutes. Leave to cool.

Beat the orange liqueur into the lukewarm confectioner's custard, and spread in the pastry case (shell). Cover with a piece of buttered greaseproof (waxed) paper until cold so that the custard does not develop a skin.

Arrange the grapes on the custard, making a second layer if necessary, and starting in the centre of the tart. Brush with the warm apricot glaze. Eat cold.

STRAWBERRY AND APRICOT TART

Metric/imperial		American
225g/8 oz	prepared sweet shortcrust pastry (sweet pie pastry)	½ lb
100g/4 oz	caster sugar	½ cup
450g/1 lb	canned apricot halves, drained	1 lb
225g/8 oz	small strawberries	½ cup

Line a 20cm/8 inch flan tin (pie pan) with the pastry. Sprinkle the base with 50g/2 oz/¼ US cup sugar. Arrange the apricots close together on the pastry base, cut side up, so that the juice does not run into the pastry. Sprinkle with the remaining sugar, then bake in a fairly hot oven, 200°C/400°F/Gas 6, for 30 minutes. As soon as the tart is cooked, arrange the strawberries in the apricot halves. Eat warm.

French Grape Tart **and** Strawberry and Apricot Tart

STRAWBERRY CREAM TART

Metric/imperial		American
225g/8 oz	prepared sweet shortcrust pastry (sweet pie pastry)	½ lb
	2 eggs	
50g/2 oz	granulated sugar	¼ cup
15g/½ oz	cornflour (cornstarch)	2 tablespoons
300ml/½ pint	milk	1¼ cups
	a few drops vanilla essence (extract) (optional)	
4×15ml spoons/ 4 tablespoons	single (light) cream	5 tablespoons
450g/1 lb	small strawberries	1 lb
50g/2 oz	caster sugar	¼ cup
	redcurrant glaze (page 14)	

Line a 20cm/8 inch flan tin (pie pan) with the pastry. Mix together the eggs, sugar and cornflour (cornstarch). Heat the milk to just under boiling point. Pour on to the egg mixture, mix well and return to the saucepan. Stir over low heat until the custard is smooth and creamy. Cook until lukewarm and, if liked, add a few drops of vanilla essence (extract). Stir in the cream, and pour into the pastry case (shell). Bake in a fairly hot oven, 190°C/375°F/Gas 5, for 25 minutes.

Sprinkle the strawberries with the caster sugar, and leave to stand. Remove the tart from the oven, cool until lukewarm, then arrange the strawberries on top of the cream filling in circles, piling any additional berries on top. Pour over the fruit syrup which has formed from the sugar. Leave to stand for 2 hours in a cold place. Just before serving, brush the fruit with the warm glaze.

HONEY APPLE TART

Metric/imperial		American
225g/8 oz	prepared sweet shortcrust pastry (sweet pie pastry)	½ lb
450g/1 lb	cooking apples, peeled, cored and cut into small pieces	1 lb
3×15ml spoons/ 3 tablespoons	water	4 tablespoons
5×15ml spoons/ 5 tablespoons	honey	6 tablespoons
	grated rind of 1 lemon	
25g/1 oz	butter	2 tablespoons
1×5ml spoon/ 1 teaspoon	ground cinnamon	1 teaspoon
1×5ml spoon/ 1 teaspoon	brandy **or** sherry	1 teaspoon
	egg white	
	3 eating apples, cored, peeled and thinly sliced	
	juice of ½ lemon	

Line a 20cm/8 inch flan tin (pie pan) with the pastry. Cook the apple pieces in a pan with the water, 3×15ml spoons/3 tablespoons/4 US tablespoons honey, the lemon rind, butter and cinnamon until reduced to a thick purée. Leave to cool, then stir in the brandy or sherry.

Brush the base of the pastry case (shell) with a little egg white, then pour in the purée and arrange the sliced apples on top. Bake in a fairly hot oven, 200°C/400°F/Gas 6, for 30 minutes. Put the remaining honey into a small pan with the lemon juice, and heat gently until the honey melts. Brush or spoon over the surface of the apples. Eat hot or cold.

CARAMELIZED APPLE TART

Metric/imperial		American
75g/3 oz	butter	6 tablespoons
150g/5 oz	granulated sugar	½ cup + 2 tablespoons
	5 eating apples, peeled, cored and sliced	
225g/8 oz	prepared sweet shortcrust pastry (sweet pie pastry)	½ lb

Use 50g/2 oz/¼ US cup butter to grease a 20cm/8 inch sandwich tin (layer cake pan) thickly on the bottom and sides. Sprinkle with 50g/2 oz/¼ US cup of the sugar. Arrange a layer of apples neatly on the sugar, and cover with the remaining apple slices. Sprinkle with 25g/1 oz/2 US tablespoons sugar. Cover with the pastry, tucking it in lightly round the apples with the tips of the fingers. Bake in a hot oven, 220°C/425°F/Gas 7, for 20 minutes.

Turn the tart at once on to an ovenproof flat plate. Sprinkle with the remaining sugar, and dot with flakes of the remaining butter. Put into a very hot oven 230°C/450°F/Gas 8, for 5 minutes until the apples are caramelized. Eat warm.

Note If preferred, the tart can be put under a very hot grill (broiler) to caramelize the apples.

NORMANDY APPLE CUSTARD TART

Metric/imperial		American
225g/8 oz	prepared sweet shortcrust pastry (sweet pie pastry)	½ lb
	6 small eating apples, peeled and cored	
8×15ml spoons/ 8 tablespoons	double (heavy) cream	9 tablespoons
	1 egg	
25g/1 oz	granulated sugar	2 tablespoons
2×15ml spoons/ 2 tablespoons	Kirsch	3 tablespoons

Line a 20cm/8 inch flan tin (pie pan) with the pastry, then chill. Prick the pastry well and bake blind in a fairly hot oven, 200°C/400°F/Gas 6, for 15 minutes. Leave to cool.

Arrange the whole apples in the pastry case (shell). Beat together the cream, egg, sugar and Kirsch, and pour this over the apples. Bake in a fairly hot oven, 190°C/375°F/Gas 5, for 30 minutes. Eat warm.

BOURDALOUE TART

Metric/imperial		American
225g/8 oz	prepared sweet shortcrust pastry (sweet pie pastry)	½ lb
	4 egg yolks	
100g/4 oz	granulated sugar	½ cup
40g/1½ oz	flour	6 tablespoons
250ml/8 fl oz	milk	1 cup
	1 vanilla pod (bean)	
100g/4 oz	unsalted butter	½ cup
	4–6 ripe eating pears, peeled and halved **or** canned pears, drained	
	redcurrant glaze (page 14)	
	flaked (slivered) almonds	

Line a 20cm/8 inch flan tin (pie pan) with the pastry, then chill. Prick the pastry well and bake blind in a fairly hot oven, 200°C/400°F/Gas 6, for 15 minutes. Leave to cool.

Mix together the egg yolks, sugar and flour until smooth. Heat the milk and vanilla pod (bean) until lukewarm. Remove the vanilla pod (bean), and pour the warm milk on to the egg yolks. Mix well, then return to the saucepan and stir over low heat until the custard just comes to boiling point. Remove from the heat, stir in the butter, and cool until lukewarm.

Pour the custard into the pastry case (shell) and arrange the pears on top, cut side down. Bake in a moderate oven, 180°C/350°F/Gas 4, for 20 minutes. Leave until lukewarm, then brush with the warm glaze. Sprinkle with the almonds. Eat hot or cold.

PEAR GINGER TART

Metric/imperial		American
225g/8 oz	prepared shortcrust pastry (basic pie pastry)	½ lb
300ml/½ pint	natural yoghurt	1¼ cups
	2 eggs	
	2 pieces stem (preserved) ginger, chopped	
1 × 15ml spoon/ 1 tablespoon	ginger syrup	1 tablespoon
25g/1 oz	caster sugar	2 tablespoons
	3 ripe eating pears, peeled, cored and halved	

Line a 20cm/8 inch flan tin (pie pan) with the pastry. Prick the pastry well and bake blind in a fairly hot oven, 200°C/400°F/Gas 6, for 15 minutes. Leave to cool.

Whisk together the yoghurt and eggs, and stir in the ginger, syrup and sugar. Put half the mixture into the pastry case (shell) and bake in a fairly hot oven, 200°C/400°F/Gas 6, for 15 minutes. Arrange the pear halves in the case (shell), cut side down. Spoon on the remaining yoghurt mixture, and bake for a further 10 minutes. Eat hot or cold.

PLUM FRANGIPANE TART

Metric/imperial		American
225g/8 oz	prepared sweet shortcrust pastry (sweet pie pastry)	½ lb
100g/4 oz	granulated sugar	½ cup
100g/4 oz	ground almonds	1 cup
	1 egg **plus** 1 egg yolk	
50g/2 oz	butter, softened	¼ cup
1×15ml spoon/ 1 tablespoon	Kirsch	1 tablespoon
450g/1 lb	small, ripe plums, halved and stoned (pitted)	1 lb
50g/2 oz	caster sugar	¼ cup

Line a 20cm/8 inch flan tin (pie pan) with the pastry. Mix together the sugar, almonds, egg, egg yolk, butter and Kirsch. Spread this mixture in the pastry case (shell). Arrange the plums, cut side down, on the almond mixture, leaving space between them. Sprinkle with the caster sugar. Bake in a fairly hot oven, 200°C/400°F/Gas 6, for 40 minutes. Eat warm or cold.

CINNAMON PLUM TART

Metric/imperial		American
225g/8 oz	prepared sweet shortcrust pastry (sweet pie pastry)	½ lb
450g/1 lb	ripe, firm plums, halved and stoned (pitted)	1 lb
150g/5 oz	caster sugar	½ cup + 2 tablespoons
1×5ml spoon/ 1 teaspoon	ground cinnamon	1 teaspoon
1×5ml spoon/ 1 teaspoon	lemon juice	1 teaspoon
25g/1 oz	butter, cut into thin flakes	2 tablespooons

Line a 20cm/8 inch flan tin (pie pan) with the pastry. Arrange the plums, cut side up, in the pastry case (shell). Mix together the sugar and cinnamon, and sprinkle half over the plums. Sprinkle with the lemon juice, and dot with the flakes of butter. Bake in a fairly hot oven, 200°C/400°F/Gas 6, for 15 minutes, then reduce the heat to moderate, 180°C/350°F/Gas 4, and bake for a further 30 minutes. Sprinkle with the remaining sugar mixture. Eat hot or cold.

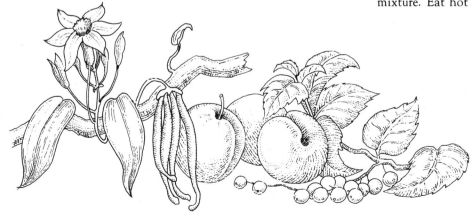

ALSACE PLUM TART

Metric/imperial		American
225g/8 oz	prepared sweet shortcrust pastry (sweet pie pastry)	½ lb
450g/1 lb	whole small yellow plums, stoned (pitted)	1 lb
	1 egg	
25g/1 oz	flour	¼ cup
50g/2 oz	granulated sugar	¼ cup
6×15ml spoons/ 6 tablespoons	milk	7 tablespoons
1×15ml spoon/ 1 tablespoon	Kirsch	1 tablespoon

Line a 20cm/8 inch flan tin (pie pan) with the pastry. Prick the pastry well and bake blind in a fairly hot oven, 200°C/400°F/Gas 6, for 15 minutes. Leave to cool.

Arrange the whole plums in the pastry case (shell). Mix the egg with the flour, sugar, milk and Kirsch, and pour this over the plums. Bake in a moderate oven, 180°C/350°F/Gas 4, for 30 minutes. Eat warm or cold.

ALMOND TART

Metric/imperial		American
225g/8 oz	prepared shortcrust pastry (basic pie pastry)	½ lb
	2 egg yolks	
25g/1 oz	granulated sugar	2 tablespoons
250ml/8 fl oz	milk	1 cup
25g/1 oz	soft breadcrumbs	½ cup
50g/2 oz	ground almonds	½ cup
25g/1 oz	butter	2 tablespoons
	a few drops almond **or** vanilla essence (extract)	
	1 egg white	
2×15ml spoons/ 2 tablespoons	raspberry jam	3 tablespoons

Line a 20cm/8 inch flan tin (pie pan) with the pastry. Mix together the egg yolks and sugar until smooth. Heat the milk to just under boiling point. Pour on to the egg yolks, mix well and return to the saucepan. Stir over low heat until the custard coats the back of the spoon. Remove from the heat and stir in the breadcrumbs, almonds, butter and essence (extract). Whisk the egg white until stiff peaks form, then fold into the mixture.

Spread the jam on the pastry base (shell) and pour in the custard mixture. Bake in a fairly hot oven, 200°C/400°F/Gas 6, for 10 minutes, then reduce the heat to moderate, 180°C/ 350°F/Gas 4, and bake for a further 30 minutes. Eat hot or cold.

NUTTY RAISIN TART

Metric/imperial		American
225g/8 oz	prepared shortcrust pastry (basic pie pastry)	½ lb
225g/8 oz	seedless raisins	1⅓ cups
300ml/½ pint	boiling water	1¼ cups
1×15ml spoon/ 1 tablespoon	cornflour (cornstarch)	
75g/3 oz	light soft brown sugar	6 tablespoons
100g/4 oz	walnuts	1 cup
	grated rind and juice of 1 lemon	
	2 eggs, beaten	
25g/1 oz	butter, softened	2 tablespoons

Line a 20cm/8 inch flan tin (pie pan) with the pastry, then chill. Prick the pastry well and bake blind in a fairly hot oven, 200°C/400°F/Gas 6, for 15 minutes. Leave to cool.

Cook the raisins in a pan with the water for 5 minutes until the raisins are plump. Mix the cornflour (cornstarch) with 1×15ml spoon/1 tablespoon water, and stir into the pan. Add the sugar, and heat gently until dissolved. Reserve 12 walnut halves for decoration and chop the rest coarsely. Stir the chopped nuts into the raisin mixture. Remove from the heat and stir in the lemon rind and juice, the eggs and butter. Leave to cool for 15 minutes.

Pour the mixture into the pastry case (shell) and arrange the reserved nuts on top. Bake in a fairly hot oven, 200°C/400°F/Gas 6, for 10 minutes, then reduce the heat to moderate, 180°C/350°F/Gas 4, and bake for a further 40 minutes. Serve cold, with thick (heavy) cream or ice cream.

BANANA AND COCONUT TART

Metric/imperial		American
225g/8 oz	prepared sweet shortcrust pastry (sweet pie pastry)	½ lb
	4 bananas, thinly sliced	
1×15ml spoon/ 1 tablespoon	rum	1 tablespoon
15g/½ oz	vanilla sugar	1 tablespoon
	a pinch of ground cinnamon	
	juice of 1 lemon	
50g/2 oz	desiccated (shredded) coconut	⅔ cup
50g/2 oz	icing (confectioner's) sugar	½ cup

Line a 20cm/8 inch flan tin (pie pan) with the pastry. Put the bananas into a bowl, sprinkle with the rum, vanilla sugar, cinnamon and lemon juice, and leave to stand for 10 minutes. Drain the bananas and arrange them in the pastry case (shell). Mix the coconut and icing (confectioner's) sugar, and sprinkle this over the bananas. Sprinkle with the rum, sugar, cinnamon and lemon juice mixture. Bake in a fairly hot oven, 200°C/400°F/Gas 6, for 15 minutes, then reduce the heat to moderate, 180°C/350°F/Gas 4, and bake for a further 25 minutes. Eat hot or cold.

PARTY PIECES

Quiches, flans and tarts make very attractive centrepieces for buffet parties. Quiches and flans may be accompanied by a variety of salads or by small hot new potatoes and young vegetables such as peas, beans or carrots. For drinks parties, small tartlets are easy to make and are far more attractive than crisps (potato chips) and nuts, and less fiddly than canapés.

For a sweet course, a tart may be served accompanied by a bowl of whipped cream, perhaps flavoured with a complementary liqueur.

SALMON CREAM FLAN

Metric/imperial		American
450g/1 lb	prepared shortcrust pastry (basic pie pastry)	1 lb
450g/1 lb	canned pink salmon, flaked	1 lb
	10cm/4 inch length cucumber, diced	
6×15ml spoons/ 6 tablespoons	mayonnaise	7 tablespoons
300ml/½ pint	soured cream	1¼ cups
3×5ml spoons/ 3 teaspoons	powdered gelatine (unflavored gelatin)	3 teaspoons
3×15ml spoons/ 3 tablespoons	water	4 tablespoons
2×5ml spoons/ 2 teaspoons	wine vinegar	2 teaspoons
	salt, pepper	

GARNISH
thin slices cucumber

Line a 30cm/12 inch flan tin (pie pan) with the pastry, then chill. Prick the pastry well and bake blind in a fairly hot oven, 200°C/400°F/Gas 6, for 20 minutes. Leave to cool.

Put the salmon, cucumber, mayonnaise and soured cream into a bowl. Soften the gelatine in the water and vinegar, and heat over a pan of hot water until syrupy. Stir into the salmon mixture, and season well with salt and pepper.

Spoon the mixture into the pastry case (shell) and smooth the surface. Chill for 1 hour, then garnish with thin slices of cucumber. Eat freshly made.

Salmon Cream Flan

SALMON PÂTÉ FLAN

Metric/imperial		American
450g/1 lb	prepared cheese pastry	1 lb
450g/1 lb	canned red salmon, mashed	1 lb
75g/3 oz	fresh brown **or** white breadcrumbs	1½ cups
300ml/½ pint	milk	1¼ cups
	2 eggs	
50g/2 oz	butter, melted	¼ cup
2×15ml spoons/ 2 tablespoons	lemon juice	3 tablespoons
2×15ml spoons/ 2 tablespoons	fresh parsley, chopped	3 tablespoons
	pepper	

Line a 30cm/12 inch flan tin (pie pan) with the pastry, then chill.

Mix together the salmon, breadcrumbs, milk, eggs, butter, lemon juice, parsley and plenty of pepper. Beat well, then leave to stand for 15 minutes.

Pour the mixture into the pastry case (shell), and bake in a fairly hot oven, 200°C/400°F/Gas 6, for 20 minutes. Reduce the heat to 190°C/375°F/Gas 5, and bake for a further 20 minutes. Eat hot or cold.

SMOKED SALMON AND SPINACH QUICHE

Metric/imperial		American
450g/1 lb	prepared shortcrust pastry (basic pie pastry)	1 lb
225g/8 oz	smoked salmon, sliced	½ lb
225g/8 oz	fresh spinach, washed and drained	½ lb
	3 eggs	
450ml/¾ pint	single (light) cream	2 cups
	pepper	
1×15ml spoon/ 1 tablespoon	Parmesan cheese, grated	1 tablespoon
	a pinch of ground nutmeg	

Line a 30cm/12 inch flan tin (pie pan) with the pastry. Cover the base and sides with the sliced salmon. Cook the spinach for 5 minutes in the water which clings to the leaves, then press out all the moisture, and spread the spinach in the pastry case (shell). Beat together the eggs, cream and pepper, and pour this over the spinach. Sprinkle with the cheese and nutmeg, and bake in a fairly hot oven, 200°C/400°F/Gas 6, for 35 minutes until golden-brown. Eat hot or cold.

LOBSTER CREAM QUICHE

Metric/imperial		American
450g/1 lb	prepared puff pastry	1 lb
15g/½ oz	butter	1 tablespoon
100g/4 oz	lean bacon, rinds removed and finely chopped	½ cup
450g/1 lb	lobster flesh, chopped	1 lb
1 × 2.5ml spoon/ ½ teaspoon	fresh dill	½ teaspoon
	3 eggs	
300ml/½ pint	single (light) cream	1¼ cups
	salt, pepper	
25g/1 oz	Parmesan cheese, grated	¼ cup

Line a 30cm/12 inch flan tin (pie pan) with the pastry. Melt the butter in a pan and fry the bacon until just cooked but not crisp. Drain well and sprinkle into the pastry case (shell). Cover with the chopped lobster and the dill. Beat together the eggs and cream, and season well with salt and pepper. Pour this over the lobster, and sprinkle with the grated cheese. Bake in a fairly hot oven, 190°C/375°F/Gas 5, for 40 minutes. Eat hot.

CRAB PUFF TARTLETS

Metric/imperial		American
275g/10 oz	prepared cheese pastry	about ¾ lb
25g/1 oz	butter	2 tablespoons
20g/¾ oz	flour	3 tablespoons
150ml/¼ pint	single (light) cream	⅔ cup
40g/1½ oz	Parmesan cheese, grated	scant ½ cup
175g/6 oz	crabmeat, flaked (see **Note**)	⅓ lb
1 × 15ml spoon/ 1 tablespoon	dry sherry	1 tablespoon
	salt, pepper	
	a pinch of mustard powder	
	1 egg, separated	

Line 12–15 individual tartlet tins (pans) with the pastry, then chill. Prick the pastry well and bake blind in a fairly hot oven, 200°C/400°F/Gas 6, for 15 minutes. Leave to cool.

Melt the butter in a pan, add the flour and cook for 1 minute. Remove from the heat and stir in the cream. Cook very gently, stirring well, until the sauce thickens. Remove from the heat and stir in 25g/1 oz/¼ US cup cheese. Add the crabmeat, sherry, salt, pepper and mustard, then work in the egg yolk. Whisk the egg white until stiff peaks form, and fold into the mixture.

Spoon the mixture into the pastry cases (shells), sprinkle with the remaining cheese, and bake in a fairly hot oven, 200°C/400°F/Gas 6, for 5 minutes. Eat hot.

Note The crabmeat can be fresh, canned or frozen.

PRAWN (SHRIMP) COCKTAIL TARTLETS

Metric/imperial		American
275g/10 oz	prepared cheese pastry	about ¾ lb
100g/4 oz	peeled prawns (shelled shrimp)	⅔ cup
	1 hard-boiled egg, finely chopped	
	1 stick of celery, finely chopped	
50g/2 oz	cucumber, chopped	½ cup
3×15ml spoons/ 3 tablespoons	mayonnaise	4 tablespoons
1×15ml spoon/ 1 tablespoon	tomato ketchup	1 tablespoon

GARNISH
fresh herbs

Line 12–15 individual tartlet tins (pans) with the pastry, then chill. Prick the pastry well and bake blind in a fairly hot oven, 200°C/400°F/Gas 6, for 20 minutes. Cool on a wire rack.

Mix together the prawns (shrimp), egg, celery and cucumber. Mix the mayonnaise and tomato ketchup until evenly coloured, then stir into the prawn (shrimp) mixture until all the ingredients are well mixed. Spoon into the pastry cases (shells) and garnish with fresh herbs. Serve immediately.

DUCK AND APPLE FLAN

Metric/imperial		American
450g/1 lb	prepared shortcrust pastry (basic pie pastry)	1 lb
15g/½ oz	aspic jelly crystals	½ oz
450ml/¾ pint	apple sauce	2 cups
	8 fresh sage leaves, finely chopped	
	salt, pepper	
	juice and rind of 1 orange, cut into very thin strips	
2.25kg/5 lb	roast duckling, carved into very thin slices	5 lb

Line a 30cm/12 inch flan tin (pie pan) with the pastry, then chill. Prick the pastry well and bake blind in a fairly hot oven, 200°C/400°F/Gas 6, for 20 minutes. Leave to cool.

Make up the aspic jelly according to the directions on the packet to make 300ml/½ pint/1¼ US cups, and leave until cool and syrupy. Put the apple sauce into a bowl and add the sage leaves, salt and pepper. Mix together with the orange juice. Put the orange strips into a small pan of water, bring to the boil and boil for 3 minutes. Drain very well, then stir them into the aspic jelly.

Spread the apple sauce in the pastry case (shell). Cover with any small pieces of duck meat, and arrange neat slices on top. Spoon over the aspic jelly, then leave until cold and set. Eat freshly made.

Prawn (Shrimp) Cocktail Tartlets **and** Duck and Apple Flan

RICH CHICKEN FLAN

Metric/imperial		American
450g/1 lb	prepared shortcrust pastry (basic pie pastry)	1 lb
50g/2 oz	butter	$\frac{1}{4}$ cup
25g/1 oz	flour	$\frac{1}{4}$ cup
450ml/$\frac{3}{4}$ pint	milk	2 cups
	1 green pepper, roughly chopped	
100g/4 oz	button mushrooms, roughly chopped	1 cup
2×15ml spoons/ 2 tablespoons	dry sherry	3 tablespoons
450g/1 lb	cooked chicken, chopped	1 lb
	salt, pepper	
40g/1$\frac{1}{2}$ oz	fresh brown **or** white breadcrumbs	$\frac{3}{4}$ cup
25g/1 oz	Parmesan cheese, grated	$\frac{1}{4}$ cup

Line a 30cm/12 inch flan tin (pie pan) with the pastry, then chill. Prick the pastry well and bake blind in a fairly hot oven, 200°C/400°F/Gas 6, for 15 minutes. Leave to cool.

Melt half the butter in a pan, add the flour and cook for 1 minute. Work in the milk gradually and stir over low heat until smooth and thick. Remove from the heat and cool to lukewarm.

Melt the remaining butter in a pan and cook the pepper and mushrooms over low heat for 5 minutes. Drain well and stir into the sauce with the sherry, chicken and plenty of seasoning. Cool completely.

Spread the filling in the pastry case (shell) and bake in a fairly hot oven, 200°C/400°F/Gas 6, for 25 minutes. Mix together the breadcrumbs and cheese, and sprinkle them over the flan. Bake for a further 10 minutes. Eat hot.

CHICKEN AND TARRAGON QUICHE

Metric/imperial		American
450g/1 lb	prepared shortcrust pastry (basic pie pastry)	1 lb
450g/1 lb	cooked chicken, finely chopped	1 lb
1×5ml spoon/ 1 teaspoon	chopped tarragon leaves	1 teaspoon
	grated rind of $\frac{1}{2}$ lemon	
	3 eggs	
300ml/$\frac{1}{2}$ pint	single (light) cream	1$\frac{1}{4}$ cups
	salt, pepper	
25g/1 oz	Parmesan cheese, grated	$\frac{1}{4}$ cup

Line a 30cm/12 inch flan tin (pie pan) with the pastry, then chill. Prick the pastry well and bake blind in a fairly hot oven, 200°C/400°F/Gas 6, for 15 minutes. Leave to cool.

Arrange the chicken in the pastry case (shell), and sprinkle with the tarragon and grated lemon rind. Beat together the eggs and cream, and season well with salt and pepper. Pour this over the chicken, and sprinkle with the grated cheese. Bake in a fairly hot oven, 190°C/375°F/Gas 5, for 40 minutes. Eat hot or cold.

TURKEY AND APRICOT FLAN

Metric/imperial		American
450g/1 lb	prepared shortcrust pastry (basic pie pastry)	1 lb
25g/1 oz	butter	2 tablespoons
	1 medium onion, finely chopped	
450g/1 lb	apricot halves, drained and roughly chopped	1 lb
2 × 5ml spoons/ 2 teaspoons	curry paste	2 teaspoons
2 × 5ml spoons/ 2 teaspoons	lemon juice	2 teaspoons
300ml/½ pint	soured cream	1¼ cups
350g/12 oz	cooked turkey, finely chopped	1½ cups
1 × 2.5ml spoon/ ½ teaspoon	Tabasco sauce (hot pepper) sauce	½ teaspoon
	salt, pepper	
100g/4 oz	cooked peas	¾ cup

Line a 30cm/12 inch flan tin (pie pan) with the pastry, then chill. Prick the pastry well and bake blind in a fairly hot oven, 200°C/400°F/Gas 6, for 15 minutes. Leave to cool.

Melt the butter in a pan and cook the onion until soft. Add the apricots, and simmer for 20 minutes until a thick pulp is formed. Mix together the curry paste and lemon juice, and stir into the apricots. Remove from the heat and stir in the cream, chopped turkey, Tabasco (hot pepper) sauce, salt, pepper and peas.

Spread the mixture in the pastry case (shell) and bake in a fairly hot oven, 190°C/375°F/Gas 5, for 40 minutes. Eat hot or cold.

BURGUNDIAN FLAN

Metric/imperial		American
450g/1 lb	prepared puff pastry	1 lb
450g/1 lb	pie veal (boneless veal for stew)	1 lb
225g/8 oz	lean pork	½ lb
	1 small onion	
1 × 2.5ml spoon/ ½ teaspoon	thyme	½ teaspoon
½ × 2.5ml spoon/ ¼ teaspoon	ground mixed spice	¼ teaspoon
	salt, pepper	
2 × 15ml spoons/ 2 tablespoons	brandy	3 tablespoons
	1 egg, beaten	

Line a 30cm/12 inch flan tin (pie pan) with the pastry. Mince (grind) together the veal, pork and onion through a fine screen, or chop very finely in a food processor. Season with the thyme, mixed spice, salt, pepper and brandy, and mix thoroughly with the egg. Spread in the pastry case (shell) and bake in a hot oven, 220°C/425°F/Gas 7, for 35 minutes. Eat hot or cold.

FLAMING APPLE TART

Metric/imperial		American
450g/1 lb	prepared sweet shortcrust pastry (sweet pie pastry)	1 lb
900g/2 lb	eating apples, peeled, cored and thinly sliced	2 lb
100g/4 oz	light soft brown sugar	½ cup
50g/2 oz	butter	¼ cup
1×2.5ml spoon/ ½ teaspoon	ground cinnamon	½ teaspoon
1×15ml spoon/ 1 tablespoon	whisky	1 tablespoon
6×15ml spoons/ 6 tablespoons	water	7 tablespoons
	FOR FLAMING	
50g/2 oz	light soft brown sugar	¼ cup
½×2.5ml spoon/ ¼ teaspoon	ground cinnamon	¼ teaspoon
6×15ml spoons/ 6 tablespoons	whisky	7 tablespoons

Line a 30cm/12 inch flan tin (pie pan) with the pastry, then chill. Prick the pastry well and bake blind in a fairly hot oven, 200°C/400°F/Gas 6, for 20 minutes. Leave to cool.

Cook the apples in a pan with the sugar, butter, cinnamon, whisky and water until tender but not broken.

Put the cooked apple mixture into the pastry case (shell), and sprinkle with the additional sugar and the cinnamon. Keep warm until ready to serve.

Warm the whisky in a small pan. Pour this over the apples and set alight. Serve at once with unsweetened whipped cream.

CHERRY MERINGUE TART

Metric/imperial		American
450g/1 lb	prepared sweet shortcrust pastry (sweet pie pastry)	1 lb
100g/4 oz	caster sugar	½ cup
675g/1½ lb	black (bing) cherries, stoned (pitted)	1½ lb
1×15ml spoon/ 1 tablespoon	Kirsch	1 tablespoon
	1 egg white	
2×15ml spoons/ 2 tablespoons	redcurrant glaze (page 14)	3 tablespoons

Line a 30cm/12 inch flan tin (pie pan) with the pastry. Sprinkle the base with 50g/2 oz/¼ US cup sugar. Arrange the cherries on the sugar, and sprinkle with 25g/1 oz/2 US tablespoons sugar. Bake in a fairly hot oven, 200°C/400°F/Gas 6, for 25 minutes.

Sprinkle the tart with the Kirsch. Whisk the egg white until stiff peaks form, and fold in the remaining sugar. Pipe a lattice of meringue across the cherries, then bake for a further 10 minutes. Leave until cold, then brush the cherries with the glaze. Eat freshly made.

Flaming Apple Tart

MINCEMEAT ALMOND TART

Metric/imperial		American
450g/1 lb	prepared puff pastry	1 lb
225g/8 oz	fruit mincemeat	1 cup
100g/4 oz	glacé (candied) cherries, roughly chopped	½ cup
2×15ml spoons/ 2 tablespoons	brandy	3 tablespoons
50g/2 oz	butter	¼ cup
50g/2 oz	caster sugar	¼ cup
50g/2 oz	ground almonds	½ cup
2×15ml spoons/ 2 tablespoons	single (light) cream	3 tablespoons
	1 egg yolk	
2×5ml spoons/ 2 teaspoons	flour	2 teaspoons
1×2.5ml spoon/ ½ teaspoon	almond essence (extract)	½ teaspoon
	ICING	
75g/3 oz	icing (confectioner's) sugar	¾ cup
2×15ml spoons/ 2 tablespoons	lemon juice	3 tablespoons

Line a 30cm/12 inch flan tin (pie pan) with the pastry. Put the mincemeat into a bowl and mix with the cherries. Stir in the brandy, mix well, then spread in the pastry case (shell). Cream the butter and sugar, and work in the almonds, cream, egg yolk, flour and essence (extract). Spread over the mincemeat, and bake in a hot oven, 220°C/425°F/Gas 7, for 20 minutes. Reduce the heat to fairly hot, 190°C/375°F/Gas 5, and bake for a further 15 minutes. Leave until just cold.

Mix the icing (confectioner's) sugar and lemon juice, and spread lightly over the tart.

WALNUT CREAM TART

Metric/imperial		American
450g/1 lb	prepared sweet shortcrust pastry (sweet pie pastry)	1 lb
450ml/¾ pint	double (heavy) cream	2 cups
175g/6 oz	caster sugar	¾ cup
225g/8 oz	very finely chopped walnuts (see **Note**)	2 cups
1×2.5ml spoon/ ½ teaspoon	ground cinnamon	½ teaspoon
	2 egg whites	
225g/8 oz	icing (confectioner's) sugar, sifted	2 cups
3×15ml spoons/ 3 tablespoons	Kirsch	4 tablespoons
	DECORATION	
100g/4 oz	walnuts	1 cup

Line a 30cm/12 inch flan tin (pie pan) with the pastry. Whip the cream with the caster sugar until thick. Fold the chopped walnuts into the cream with the cinnamon, and spread in the pastry case. Bake in a fairly hot oven, 190°C/375°F/Gas 5, for 35 minutes. Leave until cold.

Whisk the egg whites until stiff peaks form, then add the icing (confectioner's) sugar, and whisk until the mixture is thick and shiny. Fold in the Kirsch. Spread the mixture over the surface of the filling, and decorate with the remaining walnuts. Eat freshly made.

Note The walnuts for the filling should be chopped as finely as ground almonds. This is best done in a blender or food processor.

RUM RAISIN TART

Metric/imperial		American
450g/1 lb	prepared sweet shortcrust pastry (sweet pie pastry)	1 lb
75g/3 oz	seedless raisins	$\frac{1}{2}$ cup
5×15ml spoons/ 5 tablespoons	dark rum	6 tablespoons
100g/4 oz	cottage cheese	$\frac{1}{2}$ cup
100g/4 oz	cream cheese	$\frac{1}{2}$ cup
	2 eggs, separated	
50g/2 oz	caster sugar	$\frac{1}{4}$ cup
150ml/$\frac{1}{4}$ pint	double (heavy) cream	$\frac{2}{3}$ cup

Line a 30cm/12 inch flan tin (pie pan) with the pastry, then chill. Prick the pastry well and bake blind in a fairly hot oven, 200°C/400°F/Gas 6, for 15 minutes. Leave to cool.

Put the raisins into a bowl and add the rum. Leave to stand while preparing the rest of the filling.

Sieve the cottage cheese and mix thoroughly with the cream cheese. Beat the yolks with the sugar until very pale and fluffy. Add the cream, and whip until soft peaks form. Fold in the cheese mixture, then fold in the raisins and rum. Whisk the egg whites until stiff peaks form, then fold into the mixture.

Pour the mixture into the pastry case (shell) and bake in a moderate oven, 180°C/350°F/Gas 4, for 45 minutes. Turn off the oven and leave the tart to cool for 15 minutes in the oven. Eat warm or cold.

INDEX OF RECIPES